How To Analyze People

&

Emotional Intelligence Mastery

33 Strategies & Secrets for Speed Reading People, Body Language, NLP, Positive Persuasion & Dark Psychology Protection

By: U.P.P.

I0092857

Unlimited Potential Publications

Table of Contents

Introduction

Have you ever felt manipulated, perhaps by a salesman, a colleague, a boss, a friend, a family member, or a romantic partner? And whenever you call them out on their actions, they make you believe that you're crazy—that you're too sensitive, and that you have a problem. The more it happens, the more you start to believe them. You start to overthink, you start to doubt yourself and your ability to decide without their influence. You lose a bit of yourself every day as you give in to their manipulation. You start to lose confidence, esteem, and freedom. Other long-term effects of manipulation include:

1. Questioning yourself. Prolonged manipulation causes people to question themselves, causing them to doubt almost every decision they make. This is probably because of consistent blaming, gaslighting, and other techniques of manipulation. When a person is victimized, he/she feels less and less about themself to the point that they feel lowly about their decision-making skills. It's also probably the reason why the person sticks with a manipulator. Because to them, the manipulators are the only people who understand their situations and would know what to do.

2. Anxiety is the body's natural response to stress. It refers to the feeling of fear or apprehension about what is to come. It could be caused by sudden changes such as the first day of school, first day of a new job, giving a speech, and many more. While anxiety is a normal part of life, it could be dangerous when it turns into a disorder. Often, people who are victims of prolonged manipulation develop a generalized anxiety disorder, panic disorder, separation anxiety, and phobia. All of which are characterized by an extreme fear or worry about events that may not even have happened or are about to happen and/or objects that do not generally evoke fear. Anxiety disorders can be dangerous because they can cause people to make impulsive decisions that can get them hurt or into trouble.

3. Passivity. Another effect of long-term manipulation is passivity. This pertains to a person's lack of drive to become productive in life. When a person has been manipulated, chances are, they believe that they're stupid or worthless. Even when they cut ties with the manipulator, these thoughts remain and affect how they become productive in life.

4. Shame and guilt. I have seen many victims of manipulation blame

themselves for letting other people control them. Because of this, they feel "dirty" and stupid. They think about "what-ifs" which could lead to self-hate and self-blame. Often, victims resort to self-harm, even suicide because of their intrusive thoughts.

5. Avoiding human contact. Another long-term effect of manipulation is avoidance. Some victims start to generalize people, claiming that the next person who shows kindness wants something in return. This makes people asocial which could affect their emotional and psychological health even further.

6. Being overly critical. Another common effect of manipulation is being too cautious with other people. They no longer want to experience pain and shame, so they assess every person they meet, often too critically, to the point where they look at every flaw and exaggerate it. Unfortunately, this could be really unhealthy in building long-term relationships.

7. Requiring approval. When a person is manipulated, chances are, everything he or she does require the approval of the manipulator otherwise they are subject to punishment or abuse. So even after they cut ties with their manipulator, they carry this need for approval. In whatever they do, they need to be reassured that

what they are doing is correct. Otherwise, they're unlikely to act on it. Sometimes, victims walk on eggshells around people to avoid hurting them or annoying them. Even when they are no longer controlled, they still have a need to comply with others' wishes even if it hurts them or even when it affects their overall wellbeing.

8. Depression. Long-term manipulation leads to depression. Despite what people think, depression is not the feeling of sadness. It is a psychological disorder characterized by extreme feelings of hopelessness, emptiness, and grief. People with depression do not only display sadness, but they also have anger outbursts. They get irritated and frustrated easily, and they start to lose interest in things that they usually love. Other signs of depression include sleep disturbances, lack of energy, reduced appetite or binge-eating, restlessness, feelings of worthlessness or guilt, trouble concentrating, recurrent thoughts of death, and unexplained physical problems.

If any of you feel the symptoms, do not take it for granted. It is important to seek the guidance of a psychologist to determine if you need professional help.

If you're reading this book, you may already feel these signs but are not sure if they root from manipulation. If you still have no clue, let's play the "Put a finger down" challenge. The following statements below are commonly spoken by manipulators. So, put a finger down or put a checkmark beside the statements if you've heard them. If you did, write who you heard it from.

Here are 15 of the most common phrases used by manipulators:

1.   You're crazy.

2.   Look what you made me do.

3.   I said I'm sorry. Why are you still upset?

4.   It's always my fault.

5.   I don't understand what you mean.

6.   You're too sensitive.

7.   It's just a joke.

8.   You're impossible to talk to.

9.   I thought you loved me.

10. All you do is…

11. If you do this…

12. Why do you always think like that?

13. Sorry if I'm not perfect.

14. That's why people don't like you.

15. You always act like this.

How many of these statements have you heard from people around you? And how many times have you heard these before? You may think that these are just sentences that reflect their feelings but if you dig deeper, these statements affect you more. It makes you comply with their requests because you feel guilty for not being enough or for someone who has a faulty mind. If you've put your finger down to one or more of these statements and have heard them more than twice from one person, then you might be a victim of manipulation. You just didn't know it.

Unfortunately, using words is not the only face of manipulation. Some manipulators do not take responsibility for their actions. Instead, they thought of the situation to make you the bad guy. Others even deny their promises. They give the impression that they will do something only if you accomplish something first. In the end, you're the only one putting in any effort.

The most common form of manipulation is anger and aggression. If you do not comply with their wishes, manipulators often resort to physical or emotional abuse. It could also be in the form of threats just to make people come by to them.

This ends now! You're probably tired of being accused of things. You're probably sick of putting up with others' bull. It's time you learn more about manipulators and their techniques. This book focuses on the techniques of manipulation and how to avoid them by speed-reading people and analyzing them through body language. This way, you can protect yourself from Positive Persuasion and Dark Psychology.

And if you feel like you've already been broken by your manipulation, you can apply neuro-linguistic programming or NLP to recondition your mind for healing and self-improvement.

Speaking from personal experience, learning the techniques of manipulation and NLP helped me become more emotionally stable. It made me stronger to face challenges and be more discerning of people who plan to control me. Trust me, I played the "Put a finger down" challenge, and I put them down on each statement. It all came from one main person (aside from a few people in my life at the time). The worst part is, it was someone who I trusted and loved.

At that time, I was ready to do everything for that person. All I wanted was to see him happy. Even when I wasn't at fault, I was always the first one to say sorry. When something bothered me, I stayed quiet because I didn't want to start a fight. Even when I was already abused, broken, and torn apart, I stood by that person because a part of me believed that he could change. Every time I attempt to break my ties, that person would always make me feel bad because I "easily give up on challenges."

One time, he cheated on me with my best friend. When I found out and got mad about it, he said, "It was her fault and so thought you would understand because you love me and trust me."

From a normal person's perspective, the next thing to do should have been to cut him off completely. But from someone who is already manipulated and abused, I had no idea how to start a new life without him. He made me look so weak, fragile, and stupid that I couldn't make any decisions without him. Because of his manipulations, I stood beside him even when my friends and family were telling me to run. This time, it wasn't because of love. It was because of fear. Fear that no one will ever love me again and fear that no one but him will accept me because I was already a broken toy.

When I finally got out, I already had anxiety and depression. It took me months to recover from that abuse. And when I did, I said, "no more." Now, I know better.

You don't want any form of manipulation to go that far. It's best to be prepared than to be too late. And if it already has, that's okay because you aren't doomed. You can recover! So, it's important to learn how to discern its faces and techniques. If you think manipulation destroyed you already, NLP can help you recover and build emotional stability. Oprah Winfrey, Tony Robbins, Lily Allen, and Jim Carrey along with other celebrities can attest to the benefits of NLP.

These include:

- Confidence building
- Improved body language
- Improved mental and emotional stability
- Improved skills in managing people
- Improved decision making and problem-solving
- Breaking free from your mental limits.

Unfortunately, manipulation and NLP are more difficult to learn and apply. You need proper guidance and correct information. I know thousands of books have already been written about these topics but only a few offer reliable information. Without ample supplementation, learning NLP and the techniques of manipulation could do more harm than good. In this book, you will not only learn the basic information about these topics but how to apply them in real-life situations. You will also learn various myths and misconceptions about these topics that often lead people into making worse decisions. Are you ready for the first step to break free from manipulation? Let's start with body language and its psychological impact. What is body language and why is it a fundamental factor in reading and analyzing people?

Chapter 1 – Why Does the Body React the Way It Does?

Body language is an integral part of communication. Whether it's in school, counseling, public speaking, even at home, body language is always observed. Many people think that body language is a set of mere actions and gestures to help convey a point. And some say that these are mere acts that can be taught and learned. In public speaking, for example, speakers are trained to look at their audience, move their hands in relation to their points, and express their emotions through their eyes. In counseling, counselors need to display open body language so their clients would be comfortable to share their problems. Conversely, the counselors are trained to observe the body language of their clients to see if they are lying, nervous, or agitated. At home, we are instructed not to cross our legs or cross our arms, especially when talking to our parents, because it shows disrespect. The same lesson is taught in school so children would display proper decorum in the classroom.

Over the years, people have been preoccupied with calling out people displaying the wrong body language for the occasion. Only a few took time to notice its internal reasons and external implications. People neglected to understand what lies behind body language. Little did they know that behind a small gesture lies a million thoughts in one's subconscious. How is that so? First, let's learn more about body language.

Body language is a type of non-verbal communication that involves a person's facial expression, gestures, posture, head movements, and eye contact. Although human beings have been using body language since time immemorial, it was only in 1952 when an anthropologist studied how it works. During this time, Ray Birdwhistell made films of people and analyzed them to make out patterns of behavior in specific social situations. In his studies, he believed that body movements have meaning and that they could be interpreted as language. He called these basic groups of movements "kineme." In language, it's likened to us a phenome that represents the smallest speech sounds to construct words. Birdwhistell also emphasized that these groups of movements should always be analyzed and assimilated with verbal communication to reach meaningful conclusions. Over time, he coined the word body language.

Body language can be expressed consciously to convey a point. When you're saying a firm no, for example, you can disagree by shaking your head side to side so you can express your disagreement strongly. When you want to show annoyance or frustration towards a person, you roll your eyes when they speak or raise your eyebrows. It can also be applied for clarification. When pointing directions, for example, instead of merely saying "there," you can point your fingers to give more concise information.

Body language can also be expressed unconsciously, which to some people, is more important to assess. A person can say yes, but his body language could be saying "no." A person could tell you how amazing their products are, but their body language could show they are lying. Of course, when a person is trying to manipulate you, he or she would come off kind, safe, trustworthy, and reliable. They are taught to display only positive gestures. But when you learn how to look at their body language through a microscope, you can eventually see the slips they don't want you to notice.

You see, unconscious body language is brief and difficult to assess with the naked eye. This is why investigators and law enforcers replay interview videos in slow motion. This way, they can see sudden movements and determine whether the accused is lying when asked a question. Even the strongest poker players have body language slips. But you need to have a microscopic eye to catch them. Once you develop your ability to assess other people's body language, you can protect yourself from possible scams, harassment, and manipulation. Conversely, when you learn to control your body language, you can experience a variety of benefits as well.

Understanding what the Body is Telling You

Learning more about body language has various benefits. Aside from discerning manipulative people, it can also help you improve yourself, your career, and your relationships. How?

Non-verbal communication is culturally defined. While many cues are general, some could have different meanings for different cultures. When you understand more about body language, you can unlearn inappropriate and unfitting body language. When you attend a meeting, for example, and you are about to face people of different nationalities, there is body language that seems appropriate to you but is actually rude to other people. Crossing your legs could be a typical move for you but is a form of disrespect in Japan and China. The same is true when you make eye contact with your superiors. Furthermore, giving a handshake and the 'OK' sign is inappropriate to some countries. These are only some things you need to study if you want to build rapport in your career. You can imagine what can happen if you choose to ignore proper body language during formal interactions.

The same is true in building relationships. When you're on a date, you need to learn proper body language. Don't slouch or cross your arms. Otherwise, that person will think you are not interested in him or her. When you're talking to your friends or family, don't stare at your watch or they might assume that they are boring you.

You see, non-verbal cues are powerful. Sometimes, it's even more powerful than your words. This is why you need to be aware of your body language so you can unlearn what needs to be changed. By learning body language, you can create a lasting positive impression. Plus, you can convey your meanings strategically and effectively. These benefits are important in all aspects of life.

Don't worry! Body language can be practiced, much like what public speakers do to convey their messages effectively. The first is understanding body language to its core. This way, you will have proper guidance when you finally apply it in your daily interactions.

Human Reflex, Inevitable or Not?

In my journeys, I've often encountered the question, "Is reflex the same as body language?" or "Is human reflex connected to body language?" To answer this question, let us first understand the scientific explanation for a reflex.

Reflexes are automatic responses that do not require the brain to take any action. It is enacted by your body even without you thinking it. An example of this is dodging a ball or catching it. Or when you put your hand on a hot surface, and you immediately take it off. During these instances, you don't think, "The stove is hot. Do I take my hand off?" Of course, you should! Also, when you step on a thumbtack, you don't have to think about removing your feet from the ground. Your brain knows how painful it is. And in a split second, your mind knows what to do.

Another example is arm twitching or finger twitching. Remember when our phones had keypads? There were times when your thumb would just twitch as if it's texting without a phone. You're not consciously doing it, but your muscles do it anyway. That's another example of reflex.

There are two types of reflexes: natural and conditioned.

1. Natural reflex is also known as an inborn reflex. These are innate instantaneous movements that require no previous experience. These are often displayed to protect the body from different circumstances. Examples of natural reflexes include blinking, watering of eyes, sneezing, vomiting, and coughing. Other natural reflexes include salivation, swallowing, and peristalsis, which maintain body efficiency.

2. The second type of reflex is conditioned reflex. This is developed over time and can be unlearned. An example of this is typing on the keyboard of the computer, playing a musical instrument, catching a ball, and many more. These reflexes can be honed and improved. Conversely, these skills could also tarnish. An example is playing badminton. At the peak of a person's game, they can receive the shuttlecock in a split second. But as they lose practice, their reflexes become slower.

These autonomic movements do not just happen out of spite. They are caused by the interplay of thoughts and stimuli. In the example of catching the ball, your eyes see the ball moving towards you. That's the stimuli. Now, this information will travel to your brain and will create a series of actions that will make you catch or dodge it. Your brain actually worked to create a reflex. Say you did catch the ball and it caused you pain. The next time that ball gets thrown at you, your brain will know better and will make you dodge it.

Now, do you think that your autonomic reflexes are related to your body language? Let's look at your natural reflexes. From personal experience, you can observe that controlling these inborn reflexes can be impossible.

How far can you go without blinking? 5? 10 seconds? Unless you're Michael Thomas, who set the Guinness World Record for the longest time without blinking at an hour and five seconds, it's almost impossible for you to control that reflex.

The average blink rate is at 22 blinks per minute. Its purpose is to spread your tears to the outer surface of your eyes to prevent drying and irritation. It also protects the eye from dust and other foreign bodies. Many people think that blinking is only good for protecting the body, but it can also shield the mind from unwanted stimuli. Science has proven that people blink more when they are nervous, stressed, agitated, or in pain.

Another natural reflex is swallowing. People do not only swallow when they're eating. They also swallow when they are anxious. A dry mouth and throat are some of the common symptoms of stress and anxiety. This pushes the body to swallow more frequently just to get some saliva to lubricate the esophagus. These examples tell you that autonomic reflexes could be part of non-verbal cues.

In the last section of this chapter, we discussed how body language can be conscious and unconscious where the former can be controlled and the latter cannot be. Seeing how reflexes are uncontrollable, these fall under unconscious body language. This includes eye twitching, blinking, eye movements, and many more.

There are instances when people try to control these natural reflexes by fostering awareness and consciously stopping themselves from performing the reflex. For example, a person is known for blinking too much when he's anxious. When someone becomes aware of this response, they try to limit their blinking to hide their emotions. So, how then can you read non-verbal cues if some people can control them? As good as people may think in controlling their urges to respond, there will always be slips in their actions that will give them away. Even the best poker players, the best liars, and most notorious criminals give off signals that will eventually give them away. We'll look more into it in the next chapters.

The Human Body

People do not randomly move. Behind every gesture and every expression, there is an underlying reason that stems from the unconscious. Sigmund Freud, the founder of psychoanalysis, taught us that the mind has three levels of awareness–the conscious, preconscious, and unconscious. He believed that each of these levels plays a role in a person's behavior. The conscious mind contains all the thoughts, feelings, and memories you have right now or those that can be easily retrieved and brought into awareness. For example, what you ate for lunch, what you are wearing now, what you need to do later, and many more. The preconscious mind, on the other hand, consists of everything that can be brought to the conscious mind but are not currently in use. For example, what you did last New Year, who you were with during Christmas, and many more.

Lastly, the deepest and most hidden level of the mind is the unconscious. This consists of a reservoir of thoughts, urges, feelings, and memories that are outside your conscious awareness. These contain a series of repressed or unacceptable feelings of pain, anxiety, conflict, embarrassment, or frustration. Say, you were emotionally and physically abused as a child, you did not want to remember what happened because it was too much for your conscious mind. So, you buried the memories and you locked them inside, so they never show in your conscious mind again.

Even if you have already "forgotten" the pain and anguish of the events, you cannot fully keep it inside your subconscious. It's like planting a seed. Once it roots, it grows and will start to stem into your conscious mind. Soon enough, it will affect your thoughts, words, and actions, including your body language.

Freud added to his theory that communication could happen from one's unconscious to the other without involving the conscious mind. Did you experience being distrustful of a person even if you haven't met them yet? Just looking at that person could make you say, "I don't trust him" or "Something's not right about him." Though your friend says, "He seems nice. Very active and gentleman-like," you can't shake that gut feeling telling you to stay away from him.

Later, you find out that your hunches were correct. That does not make you psychic. It means that you were able to catch the subtle body language that person was giving off. At that time, you could not explain why you didn't like him. You do not have solid proof that he is mischievous. But if you learn more about looking at people through a microscope, you can support your gut feeling with reliable body language readings.

Did you know that women can read body language better than men? Although men and women can intuitively read others' body language, men usually override their gut feelings because they tend to look at the world in a more logical sense, where everything is black and white with no shades of gray. Even if their intuition is not to trust a person, they are more likely to ignore their gut feelings because they prefer to judge the situation based on what's presented to them.

Women, on the other hand, are more cautious in reading other people's body language. Hence, the expression "woman's intuition" is born. According to experts, one of the possible reasons why women can read body language better than men is their maternal nature. Women have this innate nature to understand infants' and children's non-verbal communication. They can easily discern the meanings of specific body languages such as fist clenching, kicking, thumb-sucking, and many more. And they carry this skill with them even as the child grows.

Have you ever tried lying to your mom? Well, I know most of you attempted, but it didn't work out because your mom knows every single body language you have, and she can discern you're telling the truth. No matter how much you hide your urge to talk fast or to stay calm, your mom knows there's something wrong. Often, they just pretend to believe you. But in reality, they just let it slide. Still, they are one step ahead of you.

Even if women do not have children yet, they possess this innate nature to look at body language under a microscope. They do not only pay attention to other people's words but also their non-verbal cues. This is why you can hear them say, "She was saying sorry, but I didn't think it was sincere," or "He said he was with his guy friends, but I don't believe him."

Men usually get baffled when they hear these "assumptions" from women. But there's a reason why women think like this. And it's not because they are crazy or sensitive. Aside from other things you can consider, like a guilty conscience which is a real issue. But let's say that's not what is happening and stay on the topic of reading body language. Women do know enough to look closely at other's cues. Little do people know that most often than not, these "assumptions" are correct. Body language reveals more truth than words spoken.

According to experts, learning to read body language is the closest you'll ever be to mind reading. By mastering it, you can reveal other people's true intentions and prevent all forms of manipulation. You can detect signals and red flags which could be lifesaving in the future.

Types of Non-Verbal Cues

Psychology has proven that speech only makes up about 20% of communication. The rest is non-verbal cues. This is not limited to hand gestures and eye contact. In fact, non-verbal communication has many forms—kinesics, oculesics, haptics, and proxemics. Let's learn more about them one by one.

Kinesics

This includes one's body language such as gestures and posture. These are often used to reinforce what a person is saying. It also aids in conveying one's emotions during a conversation. There are different types of kinesics.

Gestures include all forms of body movements and are further categorized into four types.

1. Emblems. These are gestures that serve the same meaning as the word. An example of this is the 'OK' and 'Come here' sign. While these are general signals, you need to be cautious when using emblems in specific countries.

2. Illustrators. These are body languages that illustrate a verbal message. An example of this is the common circular movement of the hand, which accompanies the phrase, 'over again," are pointing to a specific direction accompanied by the words, 'over there."

3. Regulators, on the other hand, are gestures that give feedback during a conversation. These include nods, short sounds such as "uh-huh," even a raise of an eyebrow is considered a regulator. It may show that you disagree, or that you're annoyed by the speaker.

4. Adaptors. These are non-verbal behaviors that satisfy some physical needs. This is commonly found in public speaking when the speaker is uncomfortable or is nervous. You may often see scratching, flicking their fingers, or pinching their arms. Be aware of some gestures that signal a weakness. Some of these include gaze aversion, hunching of the shoulders, pulling the arms towards the body,

pressing the knees together, or dropping the chin to the throat.

Posture is the second type of body language that reflects emotions, intentions, and attitudes. According to researchers, there are two types of posture—open and closed posture. Open posture communicates interest and readiness to listen. When the body is in an open posture, the back of the body is engaged, signaling positive and expanding emotions. When the front of the body is open, it emancipates a balance in the sense of empowerment.

Closed posture, on the other hand, reflects discomfort or disinterest and lack of attention. However, closed posture can also be an indication of rest, safety, and comfort. When the human torso is curved, the body is in a cycle of emotional quieting with an enhanced feeling of protection. We'll discuss more on posture in the next chapters.

The last form of kinesics is mirroring. This is one of the most common techniques to establish trust with another person. Observe couples in the getting-to-know stage. It's as if they have the same pattern of movement and speaking. You can see that their postures and gestures match. This usually indicates interest and approval among people.

Proxemics

The next form of non-verbal communication is proxemics, also known as the study of personal space. In our society, there are different levels of physical closeness appropriate to different types of relationships. Generally, there are four main levels of physical closeness. The closest one is the intimate distance, which is shared by couples and lovers, where they can be as close as 45 cm apart. Personal distance, on the other hand, is shared between friends or family members where they can be as close as 45 cm to a meter. Next, social distance can be shared between acquaintances and colleagues. This is referred to as the normal distance where you are 1 m to 3 m apart. The last level of proximity is public distance, which could be 3.7 m to 4.5 m apart. This can be shared by a teacher to his students or a public speaker to his audience.

Understanding these distances is important to establish trust and rapport with people. If you know your level of relationship, you will know where to position yourself and to converse with a person to maintain a level of comfort and appropriateness.

Oculesics
Remember when you were kids, and you were misbehaving in front of guests, your parents could not scold you because it would be inappropriate to make a scene in front of visitors. But when they look at you with those sharp eyes, you immediately stop what you're

doing and behave. It's as if they communicated with you what's going to happen if you continue misbehaving. It's the same in school. When teachers notice that you're not listening or paying attention, they give you this look that says, "there's a consequence for not listening while the teacher is explaining." To your mind, you might get embarrassed in front of the class, or you might be asked to repeat what the teacher has just said. Whatever the consequences, you don't want it. That's why you stop misbehaving and you listen intently to your teacher. These eye behaviors are known as oculesics.

Oculesics, also known as the study of our eye behaviors, is a form of non-verbal communication that decodes eye movement. For example, when a person looks up then to the right, it usually means that he or she is lying or daydreaming. When they look up then to the left, it indicates remembering something. However, before you make a final conclusion, you need to be aware of that person's natural movements because this can be reversed if a person is left-handed.

Haptics
The last form of non-verbal communication is haptics, also known as the study of human touch. Like any other form of work, non-verbal communication, haptics is also important to understand so you can interpret how people

touch you. Conversely, you can discern what inappropriate touching for other people is based on your age and culture.

When discerning manipulation, haptics is also an important factor in determining the true intentions of other people. If there is a disconnect between their non-verbal cues, it can mean that a person is lying to you or is bothered by something.

Here is a list of the types of haptic communication:

1. Professional. Some jobs require their employees to touch their clients, such as medical professions, caregiving jobs, salons, spa and treatments, and many more. These professions allow a certain degree of touch, all of which should be related to their objectives. Other than that, it could indicate a red flag.
2. Punishment. Touch could also be negative, especially when it is expressed through punishment. This includes slapping, punching, kicking, and many more.
3. Greeting. The next form of haptic communication is touching others to greet them. Examples are handshakes, cheek-kissing, and hugs. Again, these

cues vary depending on your relationship with that person.

4. Guiding. Haptics could also be used to guide people when they move. This is evident when caregivers assist the blind to their destination. It could also be evident in dancing where one person leads and uses his grip to guide his or her partner.

5. Gaining attention. Haptics could also be used to draw the attention of other people. This is evident in schools and offices when people touch other's arms or shoulders.

6. Sympathy. When people are distressed, touching them could be a source of comfort. However, the degree of touch varies greatly with your relationship. The patch could range from a gentle touch on the arm to a full-body hug.

7. Intimacy. Whether it's with a friend, family, or lover, intimacy could also be conveyed through haptic communication. Kissing, hugging, and holding hands, portrays closeness and love.

8. Lastly, this form of non-verbal communication could also be used for arousal.

It's easier to determine the meanings of touch. But how can you use it to discern manipulation? The trick is to look at non-verbal cues as a group. A person can pat your back and roll his eyes at the same time. One could pat you on the shoulder but give you a frown. A person could hold you tightly to make a point, but you see them looking sideways, which would indicate that they're lying. A person could also be laughing with you but punching your arm painfully. All of these can show their true intentions.

Don't get too excited about reading people's body language! You need to learn more about the factors that affect them. Let's get into the factors that affect body language and the hidden meanings of non-verbal cues in the next chapters.

Chapter 2: Is What They're Saying the Same to What They're Actually Doing?

How Humans Communicate

Communication is one of the most fundamental processes of human beings. It is the process of sending and receiving information or ideas through speech, writing, visuals, or actions. While communication is an integral part of being human, there is a proper way of conveying information. This includes proper use of words, delivery of actions, and presentation of visual aids. Improper communication usually leads to confusion, incomplete instructions, and miscommunication. This is why it is important to learn how to communicate properly.

Generally, there are five types of communication: verbal, non-verbal, written, listening, and visual communication.

First, **verbal communication** from the term itself occurs when we engage by speaking with other people. It could be face-to-face, over the telephone, or through video conferencing platforms such as Zoom and Skype.

Also known as oral communication, its objective is to make people understand what you want to convey. At its very nature, verbal communication is more precise compared to other types. In this day and age, for people to rely on technology, many still prefer verbal communication.

The second type of communication is non-verbal communication which is a group of movements that deliver meaning. Most of the time, these nonverbal cues speak louder than words. It shows what a person is really feeling compared to what he or she is saying.

The third type is **written** communication. It can be in the form of emails, memos, texts, and many more. Written communication is then subdivided into formal and informal. Examples of formal communication are memorandums, contracts, subpoenas, and corporate letters. Informal communication, on the other hand, would include your strands of text message with a friend, a family, or a romantic partner.

The event age of written communication is it acts as a final word. In the case of subpoenas and memorandums, the details are already stated on that piece of paper, and nobody can argue with those. They just need to comply. Another advantage is it allows people to review the information to foster understanding and retention.

However, there is a disadvantage of using written communication. Have you ever heard the statement, "Do not be afraid of anything unless it is written in black and white?" When something has been written digitally or on paper, it can be accessed and used against you. This is usually observed in contracts. The contents of some contracts could be mind-blowing. Sometimes, because of our busy schedules, we neglect to read and completely understand what we sign. But what if it contains something that could incriminate you? If you affix your signature at the bottom, they could use this contract against you.

This gives us a lesson to be wary in affixing signatures. Read what the paper says. Because once you verify that document by affixing your signature, they could use that against you when something goes wrong.

Moving forward to the next type of communication, **listening**. An example of this is a teacher lecturing in front of students. Even though the teacher basically does all the talking, there is still communication by how the students respond. The same is true during talk therapy when the client talks to a psychologist. This is made possible through active listening, which is one of the most important communication skills that people should develop.

Active listening means listening with all senses. It involves giving your full attention to the speaker by focusing on their meaning. During active listening, interest can be conveyed through verbal and non-verbal messages such as nodding, eye contact, smiling, and simply agreeing. You can also display active listening by providing feedback or clarifying the message of the speaker.

There are various benefits of active listening. First, it can help you build connections. It makes people feel that they're comfortable in sharing information with you. It also makes them feel that you are attentive, interested, and accountable, which could benefit you during interviews, courtships, and meetings.

Another benefit of active listening is it can help you identify and solve problems. This is usually observed in the workplace, where teams are faced with challenging tasks. During these instances, it is important to listen to the inputs of your colleagues so you can derive an effective solution to your problems. This technique also helps to increase your knowledge so you can make better decisions. Active listening can help you avoid missing critical information, which could make or break your career.

The last but not the least type of communication is visual communication. People are wired differently from one another. Some are predisposed to understand verbal stimuli better, while others prefer visual presentations. These involve pictures, artwork, colors, and fashion. Pictures are often the easiest to interpret because the image could already be indicated in the photo. Artwork, colors, and fashion, on the other hand, can be more symbolic. And interpretation could vary from one person to another. Colors portray different meanings. The color white, for example, symbolizes purity or innocence. Red on the other hand, could mean aggression, assertiveness, romance, and danger.

Fashion is also a valuable form of communication. Wearing a blazer, for example, is a symbol of strength and willpower. That's probably the reason why it is recommended during meetings, summits, and interviews. Coco Chanel was the first one to impose the blazer on women. During the war, men were the only ones allowed to wear them. But when Chanel created high fashion blazers for women, it became a symbol of power.

Another example is wearing white blouses for women and white polos for men. There's a reason why agencies assign these uniforms to employees. It emancipates hospitality, precision, and goodness. It makes them approachable to clients, so they attract more prospects to inquire about their products or services.

So, you see, there are many ways by which people communicate with one another. Whether this is verbal, non-verbal, written, listening, or visual, it's important to have a clear picture of the information you are about to convey. This way, you can identify the right words, body language, and symbols to use to relay information and ideas effectively. How do you do that? Let's learn some strategies in exchanging information through verbal and non-verbal communication.

Exchanging Information with Verbal Communication

Verbal communication is the primary mode used by humans to relay ideas and information. However, as easy as it is to say words, it is difficult to convey a message effectively if you don't know how. Now, I'm not going to teach you grammar or proper word usage. You can learn this from school and other sources on the web. What's important for you to understand in verbal communication is the underlying factors that make communication effective. You can be excellent in grammar and word usage. But if you ignore specific factors, it could affect the delivery of your message. Here are some factors you need to consider in verbal communications.

1. The first factor to consider is the type of verbal communication. Generally, there are four types: intrapersonal communication, interpersonal communication, small group communication, and public communication.

   Intrapersonal communication refers to your private conversations with yourself. This usually happens when you meditate or when you think. Some people debate about this topic, saying that thinking is not a form of communicating. On the contrary, it is the process of talking to yourself. This is why psychology has coined the term "self-talk," which influences how you feel and how you respond to different events in your life.

   The second type of communication is interpersonal communication which occurs during one-on-one conversations. Here, two people swap the roles of being the sender and the receiver.

   The next type of communication is small group communication. This takes place when there are more than two people involved. In this setting, each participant is allowed to interact with the rest. Examples of this are press conferences, team meetings, and board meetings.

   The last but not the least type of communication is public communication.

This takes place when the speaker addresses a large group of people—usually ten or more. Campaigns and public speeches are examples of this.

You need to understand that type of verbal communication so you can manage your time and your scope. It is also important to adjust your tone, word usage, and strategy.

1. Medium. As we all know, verbal communication can either be face-to-face or through online conference rooms. Before you speak to someone, it is important to understand the medium so you can set the tone. During face-to-face interactions, you can easily determine when people are getting bored by your presentation. But in online conference rooms, it is almost impossible to monitor the attentiveness of your audience. For all you know, your audience could be dozing off. This usually happens in virtual classrooms where teachers cannot monitor whether their students are paying attention or not. This is why it is important to adjust the tone based on your medium. Since you can share your screen in online meetings, you can utilize other forms of communication such as videos and pictures that can pique the minds of your audience. To keep them awake, you can also facilitate activities or have them participate in your discussion.

2. Language. Another important factor to consider when interacting with people is the differences in language. Many people make the mistake of using highfalutin words when talking to people of different nationalities. It makes them feel intelligent and superior. But in reality, it makes them egotistical. If you were to speak to an audience of different professions and nationalities, it is important to use clear and simple words that they can understand. Refrain from using jargon and colloquialisms that could confuse your listeners. If you were to use some, make sure to explain it to them so they don't feel left out of the group.

3. Age. Before speakers present to an audience, the first thing that they ask is the ages of their participants. This way, they can adjust their manner of speaking and their word usage to their audience. People from different age brackets have different preferences. They like different types of music, movies, and art. Plus, their fads and hobbies are different. Knowing the age bracket of your audience will give you an idea of how to reach out to them. For example, when you're talking to baby boomers, those who were born from 1946 to 1964, you can talk about the post-war phenomenon and other major events after that. This could give you the platform to gain their trust. It makes them feel that you know where they are coming from.

It's different when talking to Millennials and Generation Z. When these people are your audience, you could talk about what's trending on social media like Facebook, Twitter, or TikTok. You can talk about their cancel culture and have them participate. Then, they'll know that you can be "in" with them.

Now that you know the factors you need to consider before engaging an audience, you need to learn how what to do while speaking to an audience. Here are some techniques that can improve your verbal communication skills.

a. Don't limit your knowledge to the script. "Never get into a gunfight without extra bullets," they say. It is also applicable in public speaking. You see, even if you prepare a script for the duration of your presentation, it is important to bag other information in case you need them. For example, as a baby boomer talking to Millennials and Generation Z students about suicide awareness, they could ask you questions about trending movies and series such as the famous Netflix original series, "13 Reasons Why." This series is a platform for most students because they might associate their life with the story. Some students may ask about your opinion on the show, if the portrayal of depression and suicide is correct. If you know about the series, it could give you a better chance of better relaying information to the students.

b. Speak with confidence. If you were to engage an audience, speaking with command will evoke respect and trust from your listeners. If you express your ideas confidently, your audience Is likely to listen to you and believe what you say. Don't look down! You will look like you doubt yourself and the information you're about to say. If this happens, your audience will get bored and you become inattentive. Instead, make direct eye contact with your audience to assert your position as a reliable speaker.

c. Be dynamic. Many public speakers make the mistake of having a monotonous tone throughout the presentation. If you keep this up, by the end of your presentation, your audience would have had gone home or dozed off.

This is why it is important to have a variety of tones when you speak in public. Use your voice to add emphasis to important points. You can also add variations to your pitch to express your emotions. This will keep your audience interested and engaged.

These are only some of the most important strategies you need to consider during public speaking. Remember, what you give is what you get. If you offer them confidence, reliability, and trust by communicating effectively, you will surely receive the same feedback from your audience. It's going to be fulfilling, don't you think?

Paying Attention to the Non-Verbal Communication

If you think effective communication ends there, you're wrong. There is another thing you need to consider to relay information and ideas effectively. And that is non-verbal communication. As discussed in the previous chapter, non-verbal communication refers to gestures, movements, and symbols that convey meaning. This goes hand-in-hand with verbal communication to effectively deliver a message. Unfortunately, it could be difficult to connect your words to your non-verbal cues. If this happens, it could cause a disconnect between you and your audience. This is why you need to learn how to match your words with your non-verbal cues. How?

Here are strategies that experts use to establish command while talking to people.

1. Power pose. According to social psychologists, holding a powerful pose has

an impact on your self-esteem and self-confidence. In theory, holding a powerful pose can increase testosterone levels and reduce cortisol levels, also known as your stress hormones. If you have this confident body language, you're more likely to feel powerful and dominant wherever you are. And when you feel it, you can embody it. And when you embody it, your audience will listen and believe you for it.

How do you embody the power pose?
First, stand straight with your shoulders back and your feet shoulder-width apart. Imagine that your shoulders are opening up from one another, so they rest centrally on the body. The next thing you need to do is press your hands on either side of your body so you can easily make hand gestures to put emphasis on your words. When embodying the power pose, it is important to face the audience. If you're in a large room, tilt your body in all directions to include every audience.

2. Eye contact. Psychology has proven that eye contact with your audience can help you build the connection between them. Plus, it makes them feel valued. Another advantage of making eye contact is it's easier to receive feedback from your audience. You can see if they're interested or bored. If they feel

detached, you can amp things up and strategize to gather their attention.

How do you make eye contact when interacting with a large number of people? One of the most common techniques is to make eye contact with one member for four or more seconds before moving to the next. Make eye contact for at least 4 seconds, then proceed to another member of the group.

The second technique is the Z formation. From the name itself, look at one person from the far-left corner, then to the back right. Move your eye focus diagonally to the front left portion, then to the front right. This is one of the most effective strategies to connect with as many people in the audience as possible.

In one-on-one settings, on the other hand, you can make eye contact for 9 to 10 seconds before you break away. This way, you won't come across as intense or weird. The same applies when you are talking to small groups.

3. Hand gestures. When used properly, hand and arm gestures can help emphasize your message and make you seem confident to your audience. Proper gestures can amplify your stories and make them seem genuine

and believable. It can also help evoke feelings from the audience, especially when the topic is emotional.

To use hand gestures, one technique you can use is to put verbs into action. When your storytelling, you can emphasize the actions by showing it with your hands. You can also use symbolic gestures for emphasizing numbers, shapes, lengths, and sizes. However, be careful not to overdo it. Gesture sparingly so you do not look like an awkward dance instructor in front of your audience.

4. Movement. Moving around the stage is another way to show the audience that you are confident and empowered. It makes them attentive and engaged by your presence. As a public speaker, it is your duty to control the crowd and lead them. Moving around the stage is an effective way to do so.

Some tips in pacing:
Wait at least 3 minutes before you pace to another area. Many speakers make the mistake of moving around every 30 seconds. This can be distracting to your audience. You can time your movement every time you change a topic. This way, you're assured that three or more minutes have passed after your last transition.

When you move, do not turn your back on the audience. This could come off rude and unsettling to some. Instead, try to move forward or sideward, especially when the audience is asking a question or when you're making an important point.

Another no-no in public speaking is swaying or rocking on the spot. Instead of coming off as a confident leader, this body language could make you seem awkward and unconfident. If you do not have enough space to move in another direction, do not move at all. Compensate with hand gestures instead.

5. Expressions. Another thing that you need to consider when speaking in front of an audience is your facial expressions. This is important to emphasize your points so the audience can interpret your meaning and your emotions. Try filming yourself while speaking so you can identify where to incorporate your facial expressions. See how you look when you are happy, sad, angry, and confused. In the process, make sure that your expressions are believable to the audience.

6. Mannerisms. These are nervous habits that can detract the audience from listening to your message. If you don't know if you have them, film yourself while speaking so you

can see what they are and what triggers them. If you're made aware of these mannerisms, you can practice eliminating them. Common mannerisms include putting your hands in your pockets, using filler words such as "um" and "so," and playing with your hair or clothing.

7. Breathing. Even if your audience cannot see or hear you breathe, it is still an integral factor in portraying confident body language. When you're in front of an audience, it is important to maintain a slow and steady breath so you can reduce your stress levels. This can also help you prevent your body to revert to nervous mannerisms, bad posture, and excessive gestures that could distract your audience from listening to your message.

   It is important to warm up before speaking in public. Inhale for 3 seconds, then exhale for 4 seconds. Repeat this as often as you need until you feel calmer.

   When you're finally in front of the audience, make sure that you're standing straight so your lungs can function at full capacity. This is important so you can utilize your voice and add dynamics to it.

As you can see, verbal and nonverbal communication go together to effectively relay information and ideas. Knowing this, it is important to learn the techniques in combining these two types of communication. Once you understand these concepts fully, it can help you succeed in all facets of life, including your career and your relationships. Aside from that, it gives you an idea of how people can control and manipulate the decisions of others. Who would have thought that understanding verbal and non-verbal communication can change your life and protect you from manipulation?

Avoiding Miscommunications

Exciting as it is to analyze people's body language, we should learn our limits in doing so. There are different factors that affect one's body language. This is why we shouldn't be hasty in jumping to conclusions. You might expect people to respond using specific body language. But because of their culture, it could be inappropriate for them to do so. You may interpret some non-verbal cues as a sign of lying. But if you consider their culture, their body language might be conveying a different meaning. This is why you need to learn five examples of non-verbal cues that have different meanings in specific countries.

a. Use of hands and fingers
The use of hands and fingers to strengthen or emphasize your point is important for clearer communication. However, some gestures could offend other people in a specific culture. For

example, the OK sign, where you put your thumb and first finger together to create a circular shape, generally means a good thing. But it is offensive in some countries such as Greece, Spain, and Brazil. To them, showing the OK sign means you are calling them an a**hole. In Turkey, that sign is considered an insult towards gay people. Even the thumbs-up sign is offensive in Greece and the Middle East. To them, that thumbs-up sign means "up yours."

Next, curling your index finger with a palm facing up generally means to come closer. But in countries such as China, Malaysia, and Singapore, they consider this gesture impolite.

Another body language that could be offensive to other countries is the conflict where you brush the back of your hand underneath your chin in a flicking motion. In Belgium, northern Italy, and Tunisia, this means "get lost". In France, however, this gesture is equivalent to macho grandstanding.

Many people think that every country accepts a greeting with a handshake. However, in some eastern countries, they regard a firm handshake as aggressive, so they bow instead. In Turkey, for example, a firm handshake is considered rude and aggressive. In Islamic countries, it is inappropriate to shake the hands of women outside the family.

Other motions that could be offensive to other countries include clenching your fist, crossing your fingers, even nodding your head. In Greece and Bulgaria, the meaning of a head nod is the opposite. To them, it means no. Before you use these actions during your travels or when interacting with other races, it is important to understand their culture to avoid offending the residents and to prevent miscommunications. If you're unsure, the best thing to do is to ask them what a specific signal our body language means to them.

b. Sitting. Who would have thought that sitting could have different meanings in different cultures? When you're interacting with other people, be aware of your posture when you're dining or attending a meeting.

In the United States, crossing your legs is normal during meetings. But in Japan, it is a sign of disrespect, especially in the face of someone older or someone with a higher position than you.

Another thing that you need to watch out for is showing the soles of your shoes or your feet. In the Middle East, this body language is considered offensive. This is why in these countries, throwing shoes at someone is a form of insult, which the former U.S. president George bush discovered during his visit to Iraq in 2008.

c. Eye contact. Generally, when people look away or look down when they're being asked a question, it usually connotes lying or nervousness. But in some countries, such as China and Japan, it is rude to make eye contact, especially when he or she is older or has a higher position than you. In Latin America and Africa, extended eye contact could be seen as a challenge, while in the United States and Western Europe, eye contact shows interest or courtship. In the Middle East, extended looks between sexes are considered inappropriate.

d. Touch. The next non-verbal cue you need to watch out for is touch. While it is normal for some cultures to hug and cheek-touch people, it could be inappropriate to some. Michelle Obama, for example, broke the royal protocol during her visit to Britain in 2009 when she gave an innocent hug to the Queen. Furthermore, in many Arab, European, and Latin American countries, people are more reserved in terms of touching. So, be careful who you pat, hug, or shake hands with when dealing with other people. It might seem an innocent mistake for you, but it could greatly offend them.

e. Gender. The last but not the least factor to consider when assessing body language is gender. In some countries, what is appropriate for men might not be for women, and vice versa. In Muslim countries, for example, touching or shaking a woman's hand is inappropriate.

Another thing that you should know in terms of gender differences is their form of communication. Generally, people are taught that when a person has a high pitch, it usually means self-protection, denial, or guilt. However, you need to understand gender differences when assessing these cues. Women are allowed to have a higher pitch because of their vocal cords. Another non-verbal gender difference is facial expressions and emotions. Women tend to be more responsive when they are being talked to. They are likely to respond "uh-huh" or "mhmm..." Women also like to show that they acknowledge the speaker by tilting their head or by opening their bodies to make them feel receptive. When they disagree with you, they have no problem showing it. They could raise their eyebrows or roll their eyes.

Men, on the other hand, are more robotic when expressing their interest in conversations. They offer less feedback and encouragement. Men only nod a few times during a conversation. Generally, you might see that as disinterest. But actually, that's just how men are. They are the answer-question type of people without showing their emotions.

The same is true with eye contact. Women tend to show their interest by sharing eye contact with the speaker. Men, on the other hand, avoid it. Most prefer listening while looking down or by closing their eyes. Some people might regard this as a form of disconnect. But sometimes, it has something to do with their gender.

These are only some of the important factors to consider when you're reading one's body language. Before we move on to an integral part of reading one's body language, it is important to understand these cultural and gender differences. This way, you can generate a more accurate reading and prevent miscommunication and misjudgment. How can you make sure to avoid these mistakes?

Be aware of your bias. Often, psychological bias plays an important role in making decisions and judgments. Here are a few of them:

a. Expectation Bias. This is the process of ignoring facts and statistically relevant information when it conflicts with what you believe in. Sometimes, because of this bias, we judge people and events based on our preconceived notions about them and not the facts that were presented. For example, a person was brought in for questioning. Because of this, you already expect that they are the culprit. However, investigators have proven that they have nothing to do with the crime. But since you already believe they're the criminal, you don't care about the facts. You just want them convicted because it's what your expectation bias led you to believe.

b. Confirmation Bias. The next psychological bias is the confirmation bias, in which people seek information that will reinforce their beliefs. This is one of the most common forms of bias because of the availability of information from the web. Unfortunately, not everything you read is reliable. But because of confirmation bias, you gather every piece of information you see that verifies your point, even if the source of information is unreliable or invalid.

c. Anchoring. The last but not least psychological bias is anchoring which occurs when you're already influenced by earlier information presented to you. For example, you were taught that lack of eye contact indicates lying. Because of that, you easily judge others for it, even when facts say you should consider their culture and gender.

Chapter 3: Reading Body Movements

I'm sure most of you are looking forward to learning the different meanings of body movements. Don't fret! In this chapter, we'll talk about the most common body language and its possible meanings. You'll be surprised how these movements can reveal what a person is truly thinking and feeling. Let's start with facial expressions.

The Face

Name the universal facial expressions that you see: happiness, sadness, fear, disgust, anger, contempt, and shock. But did you know that the face can do 4000 more? People just do not notice them because they easily categorize these nonverbal cues based on these seven main expressions. If you confine yourself to this concept, it will be impossible for you to detect the real meaning of facial expressions. The mouth can smile but the eyes reveal the truth. The eyes could say, "You can trust me." But the eyebrows say a different thing. Why do you think investigators do not believe a criminal even when he says, "I didn't do it"? It all lies in their facial expressions. Even if they use a poker face, there will always be hints that give off their true intentions. Let's dig in.

Eyes and Eyebrows:

They say that the eyes are the windows to the soul and there's a reason why. The eyes give off more information than any part of the body. Every twitch, every move, every blink has meaning. Learning each of these could help you discern manipulation and lying.

Did you know that women are better at reading non-verbal cues than men? Dr. Simon Baron-Cohen from Cambridge University experimented by showing eye photos to participants. They were tasked to determine the messages that the expressions conveyed. Is it friendly, relaxed, worried, hostile, or desire? On average, men scored 19 out of 25 while women scored 22 out of 25. If you pay attention to the different eye gestures and their meanings, you could have a perfect score.

But before we discuss the different eye movements and their meanings, it's important to have a baseline. It means assessing the normal eye movements of people. This includes their blink rate, their eyebrow movements, and their eye direction. You also need to determine their culture. Are they likely to make eye contact? Furthermore, check if they have a favorite glance direction. Some people have a habit of looking at the right or at the left. This could give you cues when assessing their eye gestures later on.

Before you go straight to questioning, you can introduce yourself first and make a comfortable impression. Make them feel that they are safe and valued during the conversation. This way, they are likely to show their natural eye gestures. Once you have recorded enough information, let's move on to the eye gestures and their meanings.

When a person looks to the right, it could mean that they remember a song. If a person is looking to the left, it stimulates a visual thought. They probably remembered a color or a place.

Now pay attention if they looked down to the right. This means that they're creating a sensory memory as if imagining what it would be like to jump off a cliff. But if a person looks down to their left, it probably indicates that they're talking to themselves.

These eye gestures will help you detect a lie. If you ask a question and they look down to the right, it means that they're creating a memory instead of remembering what really happened.

You can strengthen your claim if you observe that there is a disconnect in someone's gestures. Remember your baseline. When you asked his or her name, how did their eyes move? How did their eyes react when they told you the truth? Based on this, you can tell if there's a disconnect when their eye movements suddenly change.

For example, in Bill Clinton's interview about his alleged sexual relations with Monica Lewinsky, there was a disconnect in his eye gesture and hand gestures. In his interview video, you can see that he's using his right hand to convey his point, but his eyes are looking to the left. You can also observe that when he is telling the truth, he shakes his head or nods along with the statement. But when he told the press that he didn't have sexual relations with Monica Lewinsky, he did not shake his head no. This could indicate that he's lying. It's interesting how such subtle movements can give someone away, isn't it?

There are other eye movements that give a deeper meaning.

For example, looking left or right could mean doubt, reluctance, suspicion, or contempt. But if it is matched by their eyebrows up, it could indicate courtship or a sign of interest.

Another eye movement is looking down. When someone looks down during a conversation it can mean insecurity, lack of confidence, or perhaps that person's just thinking. But before you jump to any conclusion, you need to determine the culture of the person you're talking to. In China and Japan, people are taught that making direct eye contact with someone with a higher position than you is rude. So, for them, looking down is normal.

Next is the sideways glance. The sideway glance is more common in women than men. It usually indicates interest, especially when it is matched by a slightly raised eyebrow or a smile. However, you need to keep watch on two common cues like a tilted head motion and eye-rolling. These may mean that the person you're talking to is not believe anything you're saying. It could also mean that you look suspicious and they feel uncertain, hostile, or critical.

Often, women use the sideway glance as a secretive signal. When a person of interest enters the room, they use the sideway glance to communicate with one another. Other people could also wink. In most cases, it generally means flirting or joking. However, if it is prolonged, it could be threatening and malicious.

The next eye movement you need to watch out for is when the person you are talking to keeps looking at their watch. This usually means that they are at a disconnect, that they are rushing, or they are spending too much time talking to you. If you see them look at the time repeatedly, it could mean that they have another appointment to get to. So, it's best to cut the conversation short.

Next, closed eyelids. This usually indicates disbelief or stress. This is one of the common signs that babies use to indicate pain. When you see your children squeeze their eyes shut, it could mean that they're uncomfortable or in pain. This gives you an idea of what to do to calm them down. In some cases, you will see stammering eyes, wherein the person you're talking to closes their eyes every several seconds. When you see someone close their eyelids slowly, it generally means that they're disappointed are upset about something. But during intimate conversations, closed eyes could mean a good thing. It could indicate that a person trusts you and that they're in a moment.

Eyelid touching, on the other hand, essentially means the same thing as eye blocking, but with tension relief. During your exams, you can see your classmates touch their eyes when they stumble upon a hard question. You can even see others rubbing their eyes to soothe themselves whenever they feel stress or fatigue. Other eye movements for stress include rubbing between the eyes, slow eye movements, and eyelid twitching.

Another common eye movement is increased blinking. This could indicate that someone is bored, disinterested, or is feeling superior to you. It could also be their way of telling you to go away. If people blink 2 to 3 times in less than a second, it can mean disbelief. If you do it faster, it could mean nervousness as well. But if you observe decreased blinking, it could indicate that the person is lying. In a study conducted in 2008, researchers found that people blinked less when they're lying compared to those who are telling the truth.

Aside from eye movements, you need to consider the length of the duration of eye contact. On average, studies show that the most comfortable eye contact lasts around 3 seconds. Longer than that, and it is enough to make someone uncomfortable.

You also need to learn how to measure the intensity of one's stare. This pertains to the construction or dilation of the pupils. If a person likes what they see, they are likely to allow more light to enter their eyes to have a better look. This causes the pupils to dilate or grow wider. But if a person sees something offensive because they are likely to constrict their eyes, much like what your eyes do when you stare at something bright.

These are only some of the most common eye movements you need to know that help you determine whether a person is lying or not. It can also give you cues whether they're nervous, bored, or stressed, which could be enough to know where you stand in a conversation.

Let's move on to eyebrow movements. The most common movement we see is raising eyebrows. This usually means surprise or receiving good news. However, they could also mean that someone is worried. In some instances, people raise their eyebrows when they're in disbelief. You can observe this among women. When they do not trust the people talking to them, they often raise one or two eyebrows. It is also partly the reason why women pluck their eyebrows, to make their eyebrows more expressive.

Men could also raise their eyebrows. This usually occurs when they feel protective of women. At a bar, for example, when other men are taking a pass at their girlfriend or wife, other men could raise their eyebrows to men to warn them about what they're doing.

This is different from the eyebrow flash. During this movement, the eyebrow is raised only at a split second. This is an emblem commonly used to greet other people. But then again, it varies from one country to another. People from China and Japan are not allowed to do this in front of their superiors because it is a sign of disrespect.

Another meaning of the eyebrow flash is thanking someone or giving emphasis to specific words. In some cases, it could also mean agreeing with someone. Other times, it's a form of approval and compliment, which is evident during social occasions.

Mouth

Mouth expressions are also essential in reading body language. Sometimes, even when the eyes are smiling, the mouth connotes a different thing. Once again, you need to consider your baseline in assessing body language to prevent miscommunication and false assumptions. Without further ado, here are some mouth expressions and their meanings.

A smile is one of the best body languages in the book. Not only can it make your mood brighter, but it could also mean respect, joy, adoration, and approval. While these are the most common meanings of a smile, it has many more meanings. Sometimes, it could also mean sarcasm and cynicism. So, you always need to make sure that you interpret other people's smile based on the conversation context. Matched with their eye expressions, you can see what they really want to convey.

You also need to consider how the mouth muscles are shaped. Pay attention when a person has a pursed lip. This usually means distaste, disapproval, or distrust. Next, lip biting usually means worry or stress. If a person's lips are parted, it could mean that he or she is flirting with you, particularly if that person is staring at you for a long time. This should not be confused when one's lips are protruding, wherein the upper lip moves over the bottom lip. This could mean guilt, anxiety, or doubt. Conversely, when you see people pout their lips, where the lower lip is jutting out, a person might be expressing their frustration in a child-like manner.

You may have seen people who pucker their lips wherein they form their lips into a kiss shape. This usually indicates desire. But oftentimes, it could also mean boredom, disapproval, or even distress.

Next, when the lips are sucked in, or when the person 'swallows' their lips, it could indicate that someone is thinking and doubting something. It could also mean that a person is suppressing their speech, wherein they are preventing themselves from speaking out. It could also mean that the person knows they should speak out but they are doubtful of how the receiver will react. This could mean disapproval, lying, or withholding the truth.

A flattened mouth where the lips are pressed horizontally to one another, also known as exaggerated closing of the mouth is another body language you need to observe. This can indicate disapproval, frustration, and sarcasm.

You also need to consider how the mouth moves. If it moves upward, it could indicate a positive meaning. But if it turns into a frown, it could either mean sadness, disapproval, or grimace. Knowing this, there are instances when people turn their lips up for a split second. This could mean boredom or sarcasm. On the other hand, when people move their lips down for a split second, it could either mean that the person gets your point or has a better opinion in mind.

Another mouth movement is retraction, this is when the lips expose the teeth, like showing a broad smile. While many people interpret this as positive body language, it could mean aggression or mockery. Look at the eyes to tell you which is which.

There are also instances when the mouth moves as if it is speaking. This means that a person is thinking. Also known as subvocalization, this process is often subconscious. You can see people do this before public speaking, while rehearsing a statement, or while problem-solving and decision-making. Another mouth movement is chewing, sometimes even without food inside the mouth. If this is the case, it usually means that a person is nervous about something.

The last but not least mouth movement you need to watch out for, especially if you plan on protecting yourself against manipulators, is the mouth twitch. This is a sudden mouth movement that people cannot avoid, not even poker players and expert liars. Sudden and subtle twitches, particularly on the side of the mouth, could be indicators of lying, doubt, and disapproval. If you learn how to keep an eye out for these twitches, stay tuned to the next chapter on how you can hone your skills in body language reading.

Breathing

One of the most common mistakes people make in reading body language is relying solely on facial expressions and arm gestures. Little do they know that they can watch someone's breathing to understand what that person wants to convey. But before we learn how to assess someone's message through breathing, we may need to consider if people have heart or lung problems that could make them breathe faster or slower. We also need to determine if a person is tired or feeling hot. If so, they will naturally have a faster breathing pattern. Considering these factors, let's look at some of the most common breathing patterns and their meaning.

The most common pattern is deep breathing. While this usually indicates that one is attempting to relax, it could also mean that a person is afraid, angry, excited, nervous, or attracted. If a person suddenly holds their breath, it could mean that they are angry, scared, or in pain. However, if a person holds their breath with a glimmer in their eyes, it could mean attraction or excitement.

Another common meaning of holding one's breath or deep breathing is a mating call. When a man or a woman is attracted, they usually breathe deeply. For men, the aim is to broaden their shoulders to make them look stronger and capable. For women, the aim is to make their breasts look bigger which, according to the theory of survival, is attractive because it indicates that women are capable of giving more milk to children.

The next thing you need to determine is heavy breathing. This usually indicates fatigue or anxiety. Look at an athlete who just finished a 5-kilometer jog. You can see them breathing heavily. This is because the lungs need more oxygen when the heart is beating more rapidly. Now, take note when the person gulps in air and blows it back out. It could indicate stress and anxiety. During this event, a person might hyperventilate and get dizzy. In this case, a paper bag is necessary to keep that person from collapsing.

Another thing to consider is sighing. This usually indicates relief, hopelessness, or sadness. You can see people take a deep sigh when a struggle is finally over or when receiving good news like passing the board exams, testing negative for a disease, and many more. However, a sigh could also indicate hopelessness, disappointment, and tiredness. You can assess the correct meaning of a sigh by looking at how their mouth moves. If it moves downward, it could mean a negative sign. And if the mouth moves upward, it could mean that a person is sighing of relief.

Arms

Aside from focusing on facial expressions to read body language, there is another way you can assess what other people really want to convey. The next cue we will be discussing is arm body language. The arm is one of the most interesting appendages that convey more meaning than you anticipated. But before you read them, you need to understand if a person has underlying muscle disorders or psychological disorders that may cause them to display unnecessary hand gestures such as tic disorders. You also need to consider the environment and the temperature, for it could cause people to act and move in a different way. Considering these factors, let us discuss some of the most important arm gestures.

The first one is expanding arms. This is a clever way that makes the body bigger or smaller. If the arms are cinched to the middle, it could indicate a lack of confidence, fear, and anxiety. It also aims to grab people's attention. You can see this in wrestling matches where competitors expand their arms to make people cheer for them. However, if the arms expand to make the body larger, it could mean that the person is asserting his or her dominance, confidence, or aggression in the event.

The arm is also a useful tool so people can reach out without having to move the rest of the body. This can be observed when a person reaches out for a handshake. In this case, it could mean that the person is hospitable and friendly. However, if a person holds back their arms moving them backward, it could mean hostility or fear. You can also observe people moving their arms slowly and in a curvy manner. This could mean that they're offering comfort.

The arms are also significant in shaping objects and conveying meanings. People can carve objects and emphasize how big or small they are using their arms. This is evident in public speaking when speakers emphasize their point using their arms.

Another gesture is arm raising in which the arms are lifted. If it is done rapidly, it could mean frustration or confusion. You can observe these during arguments when a person suddenly raises their arms saying, "forget it," or "I don't know."

The arms could also be used as weapons, literally and metaphorically. If you see a person's arms tighten, it usually symbolizes a spear for attacking. In communication, it usually means that a person is offended or getting angry. It could also indicate stress or pain, even discomfort. You can also observe people when they use their arms and make them look like a shield. This means that they are defensive and that they are hiding something. But other times, it could mean that they are just frustrated. This is most evident when people cross their arms. This symbolizes a defensive shield that attempts to block out the outside world. This shield acts in two ways: it either blocks incoming attacks or it attempts to hide what a person is thinking or feeling.

Thus, experts usually regard arm crossing as an indication of anxiety which could be driven by lack of trust, internal discomfort, and vulnerability. You can also see arm-crossing when people are getting impatient or when interacting with people that they don't like. This is evident when people are waiting in long queues in a restaurant or when they are waiting for someone to finish talking.

In this case, you need to identify the extent of crossing because this indicates how closed a person is. Some people display a light crossing of arms. But in severe cases, you can see how tight and closed their arms are that they even close their hands to make a fist. Common celebrities who use arm-crossing as a symbol of closeness are Gordon Ramsay with his one-arm cross and Joe Bastianich with the classic two-arm. Both gestures could mean doubt and speculation to people who are presenting.

There are also instances when folded arms could mean that a person is trying to keep themselves still to suppress any signal that indicates anger or aggression. However, you need to assess the culture of that individual. Because in some countries, when a person holds still, it means that they want to pay greater attention to you. Hence, you can take this as a compliment.

However, arm-crossing is not all negative. There are instances when arm crossing indicates that the person is ready to hug you or empathize with you. It could also mean that a person is just comfortable, especially when there is little tension in the environment. This type of comfort indicates a lack of fear which may be driven by friendship or intimacy with other people. This is evident when the arms are in a folded arm position or when the arms are wrapped around the torso. If the thumbs are pointing upward, it could indicate approval and agreement.

Arm-crossing could also indicate concentration. Take Jennifer Lopez as an example. Observe when she serves as a judge in the World of Dance and American Idol. She crosses her arms and rests them on the table.

The next arm body language is reaching forward. This could be scary to some people, especially when their culture doesn't permit others to blatantly approach them. If so, they could see reaching forward as a form of attack. So, you need to watch out who to reach out to.

If you're interacting with people and they reach forward, look at how their arms are positioned. If their palms are facing down, it could mean that they are asserting their dominance and they expect you to acknowledge it by receiving their hand. However, in some countries like the Philippines, it indicates respect. When the elderly offers their hand with their palm down, the receiver takes it and touches the back of the hand on their forehead. In other countries, lords and ladies offer their hands to their subjects so they can take it and kiss the back of the hand as a form of respect.

But if you see that a person reaches out with their arms tight and or with their hands shaped like a fist, it could indicate doubt and hostility. Other times, you'll see people reach forward gently. In this case, it means they are offering support or affection.

The next gesture is hiding the arms behind the back, so they're hidden from view. This usually indicates that a person has a hidden agenda. It could also mean that a person is hiding something, and they do not want their hands to give it away. This is why you show your hands first when interacting with others to show that they are welcoming and friendly. Otherwise, not showing your hands could make people think that you are a threat. On a brighter note, the hiding of arms could indicate vulnerability because it exposes the torso. This can signal submission or comfort.

The last but not the least arm gesture I'm sure you want to know is the amount of 'flow' the arms have. In a 2013 study, researchers found that facial body language is not the main factor that gives away a player's hand, but arm body language is. Researchers found that participants guessed the poker's standing by observing arm gestures. Are you curious about what gave it away?

According to the study, poker players that have a good hand move their arms more smoothly. But those who had a bad hand and were simply bluffing had more awkward arm movements. This could manifest in stiff arms which could cause jerky robotic movements as compared to people with smooth arms that show a natural rhythm to them. Interesting, isn't it? Now you know better than to focus only on facial expressions.

Hands and Fingers

Let's move forward to the extremities of your arms, your hands and fingers. Contrary to popular belief, there is a difference between arm gestures and hand and finger gestures. Arm gestures are broader and bigger, and these are very useful especially when the people you're talking to like to hide their hands and fingers. But if they are visible, here's your chance to determine what each hand and finger movement means.

Everyone, including you are born to speak with your hands. Ever since you were a child, you may not have been able to enunciate what you wanted but because of your hands, you could converse with other people about what you needed and what you wanted. Hand gestures are important to make people listen to you. This was proven by Spencer Kelly, an associate professor of psychology and co-director of the Center for Language and Brain at Colgate University. He found out that gestures make people pay attention to speech. In his words, these gestures are not merely add-ons to language. Rather, it is a fundamental part of it. This is why you can derive a lot of information just by looking at someone's hands. Now, let's look at some of the most interesting hand gestures that convey information.

The first one is touching the neck or face. Experts regard this as a low-power position that could indicate anxiety, lack of control, or fear. You can even see people covering their mouths. This may be a polite effort to cover someone's mouth when they cough or yawn. However, it can also be a sign of disapproval or shock. Other times, people cover their mouths when they want to smirk, but they don't want to show you. This could be a sign of disapproval or cynicism.

Another common hand gesture is touching the hands. Often, you can see people wringing their hands as if they're washing them. This could be a sign of discomfort, nervousness, or lack of preparation.

You can also see others put their hands in their pockets. This is a defensive gesture that indicates powerlessness and shyness.

There are also instances when people use the same hand gesture over and over again, even if it is not connected to what they are saying. This usually indicates self-doubt, anxiety, guilt, or lying. This is reinforced when you see the tension in their arms.

The next hand gesture is clasping the hands in front of the body. This could indicate discomfort, defensiveness, or shyness because it shows the need to protect the most sensitive and vulnerable parts of the body.

In school or at work, you can see people fidget with their fingers. This usually means that someone is thinking or that they're anxious. It could also indicate impatience and boredom.

You can also see public speakers rub their palms together. This is a way in which people communicate positive expectations. You can observe this when people rub the dice between their palms as a sign of positive expectancy. You can gather more information by assessing the speed at which a person rubs his or her palms together. When people rub their palms quickly, it could indicate excitement, anticipation, and assurance. This can be observed among salespeople when they claim that they have the right product for you. They are taught to use this gesture when describing products and services to prospective buyers to excite the buyers and make them feel a sense of urgency.

However, when you see people rub their palms slowly, it could indicate doubt and anxiety. Or it could also mean that a person is thinking.

Another gesture is the rubbing of fingers together, particularly rubbing your thumb against the index finger. This is usually used as a money expectancy gesture. It is often used by salespeople when they are asking for tips. This is also observed when people are trying to borrow money, or when they are expecting money.

The next gesture you need to consider is clenched hands. Remember when you were feeling scared, anxious, or when you were holding back a negative emotion. Chances are, you clenched your hands until your knuckles were bright white. The stronger your feelings are, the tighter your clench. Another thing you need to consider is the height at which the clenched hand is located. According to studies, the higher the location, the stronger the mood. You also need to note when the clenched hand is near his or her mouth. This usually indicates holding back what that person wants to say. Be careful not to push people too far in these cases. The results may not please you.

Another hand gesture is steepled hands. According to researchers, people who view themselves as reputable had minimalist gestures which make them use the steepled finger position to demonstrate their confident attitude. This is also known as the power position because it is used by superiors during subordinate interactions. It is also used by people with self-assured attitudes. You can observe this hand body language among lawyers, accountants, and anyone in a position of authority.

The steepled-finger position has two main versions: the raised steeple that people use when they're giving opinions or is the one doing the talking. If this is taken to extremes, it could indicate an arrogant know-it-all attitude. People who use this gesture usually convert it to a praying gesture to attempt to appear more god-like. If this is the case, people tend to be more intimidating. The second one is the lowered steeple in which that person is listening rather than speaking. In this position, you will tend to look more interested and ready to respond. Women usually use this position, especially when empathizing with their friends while listening.

The next hand gesture you need to learn is face-framing. This is a common gesture used in courtship that is often used by women to attract men. In this position, a woman will place one hand on top of the other and present her face to a man as if serving it on a platter for him to admire.

Next is gripping hands, wrists, and arms. This gesture usually indicates superiority and confidence. You can observe this in prominent royal members of royal families and senior military personnel. This shows that they are fearless by exposing their necks, hearts, and stomachs to potential threats and hazards.

But observe when the grip moves up the arm. In this case, the meaning changes. If a person is gripping their wrist behind their back, it could mean frustration. Gripping your wrist is a way to control yourself by holding your emotion in. The farther up the back this gesture goes, the greater the level of frustration.

The next one is the palm-in-palm-behind-the-back stance. This also indicates superiority, confidence, and power. According to researchers, if you take this position when you are stressed or anxious, you can observe how your mood changes and you will feel a more positive vibe.

Let's look forward to gesturing with your thumbs. A major contributing factor to human progress is the development of an opposable thumb—a thumb placed opposite to the fingers, and a willing to stretch only from the hand. Most primates like chimpanzees and gorillas have opposable thumbs but they cannot use them as efficiently as humans. Due to the superiority of the thumb, humans were able to create tools, weapons, and other complicated structures. It also enabled us to write. Hence, the development of language. Aside from these uses, thumbs are also essential to convey information. The meanings associated with showing the thumb include dominance, superiority, and in some cases, aggression. Given the history of the thumb, it's not a surprise that it denotes strength and ego.

The most common thumb gesture is the thumbs-up. This position denotes agreement. However, as we discussed in the previous chapters, be careful not to use it especially when interacting with other cultures because they might regard it as offensive.

You could also observe other people's thumbs protruding from their pockets. This usually demonstrates dominance and self-assurance. Although this can be used by men and women, it is more common among men.

Have you ever seen people point towards others using their thumbs? If so, it may mean that a person is being dismissive and disrespectful. It could also mean that the person is ridiculing others.

You can also see people fold their arms with their thumbs pointing upward. This usually indicates a defensive or negative attitude. Matched with the show of thumbs, it could mean that the person is showing that they are superior.

Legs and Feet

Aside from our arms and hands, our legs and feet also reveal our mind's intent. According to research, people are less aware of what a particular body zone is doing the further it is from the brain. It is for this reason that leg and feet gestures are very significant when reading body language. For one, the brain is less likely aware of what it's doing. Little do you know that it is revealing more than you anticipated.

This is proven by Dr. Paul Ekman and Willian Friesen in their study about deceptive behaviors. Their research has proven that when a person lies, they produce more signals associated with deceitfulness in the lower parts of their body than in the upper parts. This is applicable to both genders. People are more aware of their facial expressions because they are trained to control them, especially because it is visible to other people. While they can control the gestures on their lower body as well, they do not usually pay attention to it because it is not as visible as their face. This is why it is a powerhouse of information that you should not ignore.

There are four main standing points you need to be aware of when assessing leg and feet gestures. The first one is the parallel stance. This is a subordinate position where the legs are straight and the feet are placed closely together. It is a formal position that shows a neutral attitude. It is a common stance taught to children to show respect to their teachers.

The second stance is legs apart. This is a common male gesture that indicates a stable and immovable posture. It indicates that a person is standing their ground and is favored by those who wish to show their dominance. It requires a straight leg and your feet should be placed around shoulder-width apart with your weight equally distributed between them.

Compared to the parallel stance, the leg apart stance has a higher center of gravity to communicate authority. It is also used as a dominant signal because men use it to highlight their genitals, giving them a more virile look.

The third stance is posing with a foot forward. Since the middle ages, men of elevated position and high social status display a stance that displays the inner part of the leg. This usually indicates masculinity and appeal.

The last but not the least stance is the standing crossed legs. This is how people usually stand when they are among others whom they don't know well. You can observe this in seminars and workshops where people do not know each other. This stance is a closed gesture that indicates submissiveness or defensiveness.

Now, let's discuss the common leg gestures when people are seated. The first one is the leg cross. More than 70% of the world's population crosses left over right. This is commonly used by European and Asian cultures. Many people interpret this leg gesture as a closed body language. To most people, this usually means being emotionally withdrawn from the conversation. It could also mean disinterest and boredom. However, many people cross their legs as a sign of comfort and sometimes, habit.

The next seating position is the figure four crossed legs in which one leg crosses the other and forms a right angle to form a number four. This is commonly used by American men and other cultures who have been exposed to American entertainment. This gesture usually reflects a competitive and argumentative attitude. However, it could also indicate dominance, relaxation, or youthfulness. The downside to using this gesture, is it is offensive to other cultures like the Middle East and some parts of Asia. To them, this gesture is usually a form of disrespect especially when interacting with people with a higher position or social status.

Another gesture is the leg clamp. This usually indicates a competitive attitude. It is characterized when people lock their figure four crossed leg into a permanent position using their hands as clamps.

Locked ankles. According to studies by Gerard Nierenberg and Henry Calero, there is a higher chance that the person is withholding information if they are locking their ankles. Airline personnel are trained to spot passengers who like service but are too shy to ask for it. Attendants can also pinpoint apprehensive and anxious travelers when their ankles are locked, especially during takeoff. In another study, researchers found that out of 150 male patients observed, 128 people immediately lock their ankles when they sat on the dentist's chair. This could indicate that they're uncomfortable or they are anxious about the procedure. This is also evident when interviewing people during investigation. In recordings, law enforcers review how the interviewees lock their ankles. This usually indicates that they're uncomfortable, withholding information, scared, or guilty.

However, there is a woman variant of the locked ankles wherein the knees are held together, and their hands are resting side by side or on top of their leg. This usually has the same meaning such as anxiety or apprehension.

The next leg gesture is entwining the legs which is more common to women than men. One leg entwining the other and the top of the foot locking itself to the other leg is a classic gesture made by women. Despite what people think this leg body language usually indicates insecurity no matter how relaxed the legs are. It could also mean shyness and reservations. Studies show that people meeting in a group for the first time usually stand with their arms and legs crossed. But as rapport develops and people become more comfortable with one another, you can observe that they release their closed pose and resort to a more open body language.

Another body language you can observe in women is the seated parallel legs. Only a few men can do this position because they do not have the same bone structure which enables them to sit in this manner. When women assume this position, they're projecting a strong feminine signal. When one leg is pressed against the other, it gives the legs a healthier and more youthful look which makes the woman more appealing. Even modeling classes teach this posture to women.

Another body language is the high heels effect. Women instinctively know the effects of wearing high heels. They feel more powerful and more attractive. High heels make the legs look more toned, giving the illusion of better health and more fertility, which according to the theory of survival, is more attractive to men. Using high heels also accentuates the arch on the lower back and contracts that will use muscles to make to make the hips wider and more attractive. All of these characteristics are consistent with the increase in fertility which has a direct relationship with attractiveness.

Then there's putting your foot forward. When you're interested in the conversation or in a person, you usually put your best foot forward to shorten the distance between you and the person. But if you're disinterested or unmotivated by someone, you can observe yourself put a foot back.

You can also observe other people fidget their feet. This usually indicates impatience and boredom. It gives you the signal that they don't want to be there or that they are waiting for the conversation to be over so they can flee. In a standing position, you can observe people tapping their foot to indicate their impatience. But if they are seated with their legs crossed, the hanging foot could twitch up and down or back and forth.

There you have it. These are only some of the most important body languages that you need to learn for better communication and to avoid deception and miscommunication. Again, before you start reading other people's body language, you need to have a baseline. Learn as much as you can about them particularly their culture, their mannerisms, and habits. From this baseline, you can see what deviates from their normal actions.

In the next chapter, we will discuss seeing body language as a whole or as a cluster. If you think individual gestures are powerful, wait until you can read them as a whole. This way, you can have clearer information on what they really want to convey.

Chapter 4 – Seeing Body Language as a Whole

In the previous chapters, we have discussed how posture plays a role in nonverbal communication. It is a type of body language that reflects emotions, intentions, and attitudes. Having a good posture is advantageous particularly in communicating and interacting. It's safe to say that it can make or break your ability to make a good first impression on other people. This is evident among public speakers and people with authority. What do you think would happen if a public speaker was slouching and had hunched shoulders? You probably would not pay attention to what he or she had to say because you'd be under the impression that the speaker was unconfident about themselves and the information they are about to convey. But imagine if that speaker owned the stage confidently. I imagine that you would be in awe and you would be captivated by how he or she commanded the audience. That is one example that shows how posture is important in communicating with other people.

Conversely, when you're the public speaker and you show that you're timid by putting your hands in your pockets or putting your hands behind your back, you are giving your audience the impression that you're not believable. It means that you lack confidence in that you're doubting what you're about to say. If this happens, the audience is at a disconnect. It will be difficult for you to command the room. Because of this, you'll see people sleeping, eating, or going out which will make you feel very uncomfortable. This is why it is very important to learn about body language, particularly posture. This way, you can make people listen to you and you will earn the respect you deserve when conversing with others.

In this chapter, we will discuss how to read posture by reading body language from all body parts as a whole. This way, you can gather more precise information from other people. But before we discuss more about posture, let's understand what affects it. These factors will also contribute to your baseline in reading posture as a form of non-verbal communication.

According to research, there are four main factors that affect one's posture. The first one is habit. Notice how most office workers have a curved spine. This is usually because of sitting at the office all day. The spine can be molded by office chairs and the screens tend to draw the face in. This usually causes the habit of slouching.

Another reason is repetitive movements. Sometimes, how we use our muscles makes a difference in our posture. For example, laborers who overuse their trapezius and deltoid muscles tend to have a misaligned spine because of the load they carry for long periods of time.

Next is injury. When a person has experienced an injury, the tendency is you don't want to move the same muscle as you did before. It could be due to phantom pain or trauma. You just don't want to inflict the same pain on the same body part. Or it's possible that you are no longer used to using the same muscle because of the length of recovery time. This is evident when people break one leg. Even if it fully recovers, they are so used to moving more weight on the healthy leg and they keep on doing it even after recovery.

The next reason why some people have bad posture is past surgeries. Most surgeries cause permanent scar tissue, which affects the proper movement of muscles. This is why they use other muscles more, which could affect posture. In this case, chances are, people will need more hours of therapy. And unfortunately, some people carry on with this posture for a lifetime. If their posture gets too bad, it could lead to other physical complications like lack of bone and muscle support, obstructed blood flow, decreased flexibility, indigestion, decreased balance, and persistent body pains.

To many of us who did not have an injury or did not experience surgery, there is a greater chance for us to better our posture not only for communication but also for physical health. Knowing this, let's start with the two kinds of body posture: the dynamic posture and the static posture. How are they different from one another?

Expressing with Posture

Dynamic Posture

Dynamic posture refers to the position of the body while it is in motion like when you're walking, running, picking something up, or bending over. It is literally any motion. Did you know that when you are doing typical things, it is still important to maintain a good dynamic posture? Particularly when you are walking, it is important to watch the alignment of your neck, mid-back, and low-back and straighten it. This way, you can maintain a good posture.

Static Posture

On the other hand, a static posture is how you hold yourself together when you're not moving like when you're sitting, standing, or sleeping. Like the dynamic posture, it is important to align your body to maintain a good posture properly. How do you do that? Let's start by determining what makes a good posture.

What is the key to a good posture?

According to researchers, the key to a good posture is the positioning of the spine. A correct posture should maintain the curves on your neck, mid-back, and low-back. Your heart should be directly above your shoulders and the top of your shoulder should be directly over the hips.

If you want to have the ideal posture, the line of gravity should pass through specific points of the body. This can be evaluated using a plumb line to assess the midline of the body.

This line should pass through an ear lobe, then the shoulder joint, to the hip joint, and through the greater trochanter of the femur. Then, it should pass slightly through the anterior to the midline of your knee joint. And lastly, it passes through the anterior to the lateral malleolus.

When you view your posture from either the front or the back, the vertical line passing through the body's center of gravity should bisect the body into two equal halves. In the process, the body weight should be distributed evenly between the two feet.

When assessing posture, you should also consider head alignment, the cervical, thoracic, and lumbar curvature, the shoulder level symmetry, pelvic symmetry, and hip, knee, and ankle joints.

You can also assess posture while sitting. In this case, consider the following criteria:

- The person's ears should be aligned with the shoulders and the shoulders should align with the hips.
- The shoulders should be relaxed, especially when the elbows are close to the sides of your body.
- The angle of your hips, elbows, and knees should be approximately 90 degrees.
- The feet are flat on the floor.
- Your forearms are parallel to the floor and your wrists should be straight.
- The feet should rest comfortably on a surface.

Types of standing posture

If you saw that there is a misalignment of your posture, you could classify it into one of these examples of all the postures.

1. Lordotic posture. Lordosis is characterized by the normal inward curvature of the spine. When this curve

is exaggerated, it is usually referred to as hyperlordosis wherein the pelvis is usually tilted anteriorly.

2. Sway Back Posture. In this posture, there is a forward head and the hyperextension of the cervical spine. You can also observe flexion of the thoracic spine, lumbar spine extension, posterior tilt of the pelvis, hip, and knee hyperextension, and the ankle slightly plantarflexed.

3. Flatback posture. If you have this posture, you can observe that there is a forward head and extension of the cervical spine. You can also see an extension of the thoracic spine, loss of lumbar lordosis and posterior pelvic tilt.

4. Forward head posture. This describes the shift of the head forward with the chin poking out. This posture is usually caused by increased flexion of the lower cervical spine and your upper thoracic spine with increased extension of the upper cervical spine and the extension of the occiput on C1.

5. Scoliosis. This is one of the most common posture faults. This is characterized by a deviation of the normal vertical line of the spine where you can observe a lateral curvature and rotation of the vertebrae. Doctors can diagnose scoliosis when there is at least 10° of spinal angulation on the posterior-

anterior radiograph associated with vertebral rotation.

6. Kyphosis. The last but not the least type of faulty posture is Kyphosis. This is characterized by an increased convex curve observed in the thoracic or sacral regions of the spine.

Do not take any of these faulty posture types for granted for these can cause major disability in the body. If you observe that you have faulty posture, it is always best to consult your doctor about the best approaches to make it better.

Still, the best way you can prevent any of these faulty postures is to improve it as much as possible.

You might be thinking, "What if it's already a habit of mine to slouch while walking?"

Well, the answer lies in awareness. You need to be aware that you have that kind of posture so you can straighten it as much as you can. With practice, you will observe improvements in how your body stance changes over time. When you're washing the dishes, for example, be aware of your posture. When you feel like you're resorting back to a slouching position, correct your posture right away.

Another technique to improve your posture is to remain active. Even if your job allows you to sit in front of the computer all day, it is important to make time for other activities such as exercise, yoga, or tai chi. These exercises are helpful to keep your muscles strong enough to support your body.

The next thing you can do is to maintain a healthy weight. According to experts, extra weight can affect how your bone structure supports your body. It's partly the reason why people have poor posture. According to experts, men should not have a waistline exceeding 37 inches while women should not have a waistline exceeding 31.5 inches. If this happens, not only will you have poor posture but you'll also experience other disadvantages like diabetes, obesity, and heart problems. As much as possible, maintain a healthy diet and do regular exercise.

Also, consider wearing comfortable shoes rather than high heels. There are instances when high heels can throw you off your balance and can make you walk differently. This puts more stress on your muscles, and it can harm your posture. If you're wondering how you can improve your posture while standing or walking, here are strategies you can use.

The first one is to stand straight and tall. Always remember to keep your shoulders back. It also helps to pull your stomach in. Next, put your weight mostly on the balls of your feet then let your arms hang down your sides naturally. If you make this a habit, you can observe the improvement in your posture and your stature.

The last but not the least technique to improve your posture is to make your work surfaces suitable for your posture. When you're working in front of the computer all day, the height of your table should be just right for your shoulders and arms to relax. If not, it will affect your posture tremendously. You can adjust your table or your chair to reach that comfortable position. If you're at the office all day and you want to improve your posture, you can switch your sitting positions often. You can also take brief walks in between work to rest and straighten your spine. Also, as much as possible don't cross your legs because it can affect the curvature of your lower back. Lastly, make sure that your back is supported.

There are also specific techniques recommended when sleeping. You need to make your bed suitable for the improvement of your posture. If you are experiencing body pains, psychotherapists usually recommend a firmer mattress so you can lie down comfortably and so you can straighten your spine. The ideal posture when lying down is to let your legs roll outward while the pubis rises as high as the navel. Your lower back should also sink down to the floor. Next, your arms should roll inward with your palms back. Then, allow your neck to flatten so your throat shortens. Lastly, position your head down and forward to relax your neck and shoulders.

Now that we have established what the ideal posture is and how you can improve it, it's time to put it to work by making it a part of our body language. Both dynamic and static posture plays a role in establishing a connection with people. Matched with the movements and gestures made by other body parts such as your arms, legs, and head, you can identify if you are open or closed to people and their ideas. Let's start by identifying the two types of posture in relation to body language: closed and open.

2 Forms of Posture

Closed Posture

Despite what people think, closed posture does not merely indicate hostility, anxiety, or lack of confidence. Everyone resorts to a closed posture in which the body closes, and the back of the body opens. It is the default position for rest, nurturance, and safety. Aside from feeling anxious, it could indicate that a person is relaxed or comfortable. According to psychology, the C-curve shape of the torso in this position is effective for psycho-emotional quieting and enhanced feelings of protection.

When we feel afraid, threatened, angry, or sad, something in our mind triggers and starts a pre-program stress reflex toward a closed posture. When we feel these negative emotions, it triggers a stress response, which tightens the body and mind toward the C-curve to protect itself. This unconscious reflex is also commonly known as the "red light reflex" and the "startle response". It is also widely known as the "slumping reflex", common in all animals that signal a protective posture to danger, distress, and negativity. All somatic areas on the front of the body, such as the pelvic floor, belly, heart, mouth, and throat are shortened and closed when you are feeling emotions.

According to psychology, unresolved negative emotions like anger, bitterness, and resentment are strong emotional energies stuck in the past. In addition, fear and worry are emotions of the future where people have reduced control. Suppose negative emotions are not released healthily. In that case, they can stay buried in the cellular fabric of the body-mind as reverberating memories for many years. Unfortunately, if these remain unresolved, it could lead to various psychological illnesses such as depression, anxiety, eating disorders, posttraumatic stress disorders, phobia, and many more.

To prevent the body from feeling these emotions, physical contraction of the front of the body occurs to suppress painful feelings and thoughts. Wilhelm Reich named this phenomenon of emotional contraction "armoring." While this is effective to bury unwanted thoughts, it could lead to distorted memories.

The common form of a closed posture is the fetal position, also known as the most primal or default position of mankind. The more your back is disengaged, the more it is optimized for comfort and relaxation.

When the body is in a C-curve position, you can observe that the legs are bent in towards the torso, so the tail is tucked under and the belly is shortened. You can also observe the flattening of the lower back and the rounding of the upper back. In this position you can also see that the chest is drawn in and the arms are bent inward so the shoulders are drawn forward. Lastly, you can see the head bow so that the neck and the throat shorten and contracts into the shoulders.

Open Posture

Now that we have established the closed posture and its forms, let us discuss the open posture which is expressed during waking hours for optimal body functioning. When the body is in an open posture, it makes it ready for daily activities such as walking, running, and lifting. The open posture is activated when the back of the body is engaged, and the ribcage is fully expanded. It is a symbol of positivity, hospitability, and expression. It emancipates a sense of empowerment that allows people to take on tasks for the day.

When the body is in an open posture, you can often observe them extend their arms forward and up, their head rises up and back and releases the throat from constriction. You can also see that the chest and heart are wide open. Also, the belly is long and relaxed. In the lower body, you can see that the knees are slightly bent, and the pelvis is tipped forward, opening the pelvic floor.

This is also known as the Bowspring position. This is evident among babies around three to six months old when they love to lie on their bellies. During this position, they display a natural engagement of their extensor muscles on the entire back of the body, allowing the baby to lift his or her head upward, arch their back, and extend their arms and legs out like a skydiver during a freefall.

In this position, there is reduced emotional guarding or armoring in the body and mind. Hence, babies seem more vulnerable. In an open posture, one's vital energy flows without obstruction in waves throughout the entire body, from head to toe.
This is why psychologists often recommend combining a positive mindset with the

Bowspring dynamic posture to clear negative emotional energies and replace it with harmonious and joyful emotional energies.

When determining one's posture, it is impossible to do it when you are so close to the person. This is the reason why experts recommend a specific distance to interact properly with body language and posture. So how far should we be?

How Far Should We Be?

As we have discussed in the previous chapters, and proxemics refers to the distance between two people as they interact. It also describes one's perception of and use of space—how much space they take up and how they distance themselves from other people. Proxemics is developed by anthropologist Edward T. Hall. He discussed that there are four main levels of distance depending on the relationship of the people interacting.

1. **Intimate distance shared by couples: 16-18 inches**
   Despite what people think, intimate distance is not only used by couples who are seeking love and affection from one another. It can also be used during interrogations. According to research, when law enforcers invade the privacy of their suspects, they can provoke anxiety

and an adrenaline rush that pushes people to confess.

Intimate distance is also used in sports. According to sports psychologists, teammates have much higher rates of touch than average friends. They pat each other on the head and sometimes on the back or shoulders to show congeniality. They also maintain smaller distances between each other. This can be observed when they stand close together and huddle on the sidelines.

There are also instances when intimate distance is used in men's urinals. Did you know that men have an unwritten rule not to speak to each other while they are in the urinal? An article published in Metro specifically states the number one rule is not to talk to others while peeing, no matter the location. It is because men need more security when they are using the urinal. They take longer to urinate when other people are standing close to them.

The same is true when riding an elevator. When people are close to one another, especially when the elevator is at full capacity, there are rules that you need to abide by. An example is avoiding eye contact with other people. It is also essential to maintain a poker face to avoid awkward scenarios. Some even recommend keeping an eye on the floor numbers as they change. If you have a phone or newspaper, it is recommended you focus on it rather than your surroundings.

Almost 70% of the population is unaware of these rules. However, others break them profusely just to irritate other people, which is completely uncomfortable on their end. The reason why these rules exist is to avoid invading each other's privacy.

An example of this is the 2000 presidential debate between George W. Bush and Al Gore when Gore invaded Bush's space by acting with what he thought was a power move. Unfortunately, his actions made him look like a bully and the situation became awkward very quickly.

Fortunately for Bush, his reactions were on fire. He stopped talking and nodded towards Gore's direction to acknowledge his action and it made people laugh.

2. **Personal distance shared by close friends and family: 1.5 to 4 feet**
    According to psychology, this is the best distance to build rapport. However, in using this distance, you need to consider gender differences. Females tend to talk more closely with other people while males prefer to have more distance.

    But did you know that females are approached more closely than men? This is because as boys, they're given toys that take up space such as balls, cars, and trains. Young girls, on the other hand, are given dolls and playhouses which take up less space.

    In considering personal space, height plays a role too. In a 2019 study, researchers have found that taller people are more likely to invade personal space than shorter people. In theory, taller people feel more dominant, especially when interacting with smaller individuals.

    If you're planning to use personal distance to build rapport but you are hesitant because you don't want to come off rude to other people, you can ask your client if you can sit near him or her. It's the safest way to determine how comfortable a person is while interacting with you. But whatever you do, always respect their personal space. Do not stand too close to them or they will feel very uncomfortable no matter how good your body language is.

However, if you stand too far, you could cause a disconnect which is also detrimental to your objective. Consider the 1992 presidential debate between George H.W. Bush and Bill Clinton, the latter was asked a question from a person who was far out in the audience.

He remedied the problem by going to the speaker to communicate with him better. This made a significant impact since she can see him closer and get a stronger emotional connection than when he was further away. George H.W. Bush didn't get the same significant effect since he remained away from the audience.

One of the best approaches to build rapport with other people is applying Navarro's "Shake and Wait" approach. This can help you determine the appropriate physical distance in a conversation in 4 steps:

The first one is to lean in, of course considering personal distance and its limits. Next, give an appropriate handshake. Third, make good eye contact and then take a step back and wait for their reaction.

If the person remains in place, it means that they are comfortable with the distance. But if they take a step back or turn slightly away, they might need more space from you. Lastly, if they take a step closer, it could mean that they're favorable toward you.

3. **Social distance shared by acquaintances: 4 to 12 feet**
This is the distance where strangers stand with one another, and it is commonly observed during formal business and social events. This is a neutral approach that doesn't really work well in terms of building relations. If you are in this zone, as much as possible, try getting a little closer and gauging a person's reaction. Are they receptive and warm, or do they immediately close off?

4. **Lastly, public distance used in public speaking: 12 to 25 feet.**

You can use these guidelines to determine how to distance yourself while interacting with other people. When they assert themselves deep into your comfort zone it might be time to call for help or to stay away from that person.

An example of proxemics is how a therapist and a client position themselves. During these situations, it is important to consider proxemics, especially when a person has underlying psychological illnesses. If you observe the proper proxemics, it can make the client feel safer. Plus, it could also protect the therapist in case the client goes amuck. The therapist will then need to demonstrate a proper sitting position with the client to ensure a comfortable position for both parties.

According to Edward Hall, proxemics is influenced by cultural factors. Children usually learn proxemics from their parents the same way they learn how to speak. Therefore, when assessing proxemics, it is important to identify what culture the person comes from. This way, you will know how to give respect to their personal space and how to understand the idea and the belief behind the behavior. Being able to comprehend what is near and far to other people prevents miscommunication and promotes rapport and better business relationships.

No matter how good you are at showing body language, it is useless if you don't know how to distance yourself from other people. So how will you master the four zones of proxemics?

The first thing to remember is not everyone stands the same even if there is a guideline, that is the four zones. Some people regard the intimate distance as too far or too near. Some regard the personal distance as too far. For example, contact cultures such as Latin America prefer to be closer than noncontact countries like East Asian and American countries. Country farmers and other people belonging to rural areas prefer standing farther back from one another. This is in contrast with city dwellers who are so used to standing close to one another because there is less space. This is explained by Edward Hall when he said that proxemics is not only used in communication but also in how communities arrange their town and their houses. In rural areas, houses are further from each other hence there is much more space. This is why people are used to interacting farther away from each other. In the city, on the other hand, people are used to a crowded space. This is why they don't usually mind sitting or standing so close to one another especially inside trains or other crowded areas.

Hall also considered biometrics as a form to categorize, explain, and explore how people connect in space. He used kinesthetic factors, haptic code, visual code, thermal code, olfactory code, and voice loudness in his book. Let's discuss each one by one.

1. **Kinesthetic factors.**
   Kinesthetic communication is a basic form of language that human beings use to interact with one another. In relation to proxemics, this category deals with how close people are to touching.

2. **Haptic code**
   Next is the haptic code, a behavioral category concerning how participants touch one another, holding, feeling, prolonged holding, spot touching, pressing against, or not touching at all.

3. **Visual code**.

   This category indicates the amount of eye contact between participants. This ranges from eye-to-eye contact, to a prolonged gaze, or no eye contact at all.

4. **Thermal code**

   This category refers to the amount of body heat that each participant receives from another. It could refer to the conducted heat detected, radiant heat detected, heat probably detected, and no heat detection.

5. **Olfactory code**

   This category connotes the kind and degree of odor detected by each participant from the other.

6. **Voice loudness**

   This category deals with the vocal effort used in speech. Some of the categories of voice loudness include silent, very soft, soft, normal, normal (high), loud, and very loud. Loudness is one of the most important factors to consider when interacting with others.

   Aside from the loudness of your voice, your tone conveys a much deeper meaning. Let's learn more in the next section.

Listening Closely

Indeed, people listen to your words, but they react to your tone. According to Daniel Day-Lewis, the human voice is a deep reflection of character. He emphasized how impactful a person's tone can be. According to him, one's own voice and tone come from the depths of one's being. Hence, it is almost impossible to fake. This is why when interacting with other people, the tone is one of the number one factors to consider in deriving and conveying meaning.

According to the dictionary, tone refers to the motivation of pitch, vocal strength, and quality that can add meaning to a word, sentence, or phrase. This is a part of a person's paralanguage which constitutes pitch, amplitude, pauses, and hesitations between words. Don't underestimate the power of tone because it can make or break the rapport you are trying to build with other people. This usually reflects the attitude or the feelings that are associated with the message. It helps you build the tone of the event, which could help you communicate more effectively.

Aside from these advantages, focusing on your tone helps you build authority and command. Imagine going to the stage and speaking to the crowd with a soft voice. Much like having a closed posture, people are less likely to take you seriously. It will be difficult for you to establish your authority and to make people listen to what you're about to say. According to experts, it is important to own the stage with your presence in with your voice. As much as possible, do not speak in a monotonous tone. Maintain a fun and lively tone to keep your audience engaged.

Another advantage of studying tone is you can assess what other people really want to convey despite the words they say or the body language they show. However, before you study and assess one's tone, you need to consider cultural differences. In some countries, they talk loudly as if they are shouting. But in their culture, that is the normal way of interacting with other people. In contrast, some cultures have very soft tones. So, even if they're angry you cannot tell because of the softness and tenderness of their voice. Before you interact with people of different cultures, you need to have that baseline and determine the normal tone of their voice. This way, you can avoid miscommunication and misinterpretation.

Once you've created that baseline, it is time to assess the different meanings of a person's tone in public speaking. Let's start on one's pitch.

Pitch
Pitch is an important auditory attribute of sound ordered on a scale from low to high. Think about the notes on a melodic score. This will show you how pitch works. When observing one's pitch, you need to consider gender differences. Generally, females have a higher pitch than males.

> **Informational:** When the pitch is in a normal spectrum, it usually means that a person is conveying information. This pitch is

somewhat monotonous, but it goes down the spectrum from time to time.

Grammatical: This is observed by the rising pitch, which turns a statement into a yes-no question, such as "He's going ↗home?"

Illocution: The pitch pattern characterizes the intentional meaning, for example, "Why ↘don't you move to California?" which connotes a question, versus "Why don't you ↗move to California?" which signals a suggestion.

Attitudinal: A declining pitch signal characterizes this. Instead of "Good ↗morn↘ing" which indicates excitement or joy, versus "Good morn↘ing," which demonstrates attitude or superiority.

There are also instances when a person speaks in a higher pitch than usual. This usually means anxiety, nervousness, lying, denial, or withholding the truth. Sometimes you can also observe other people speak in a lower pitch than usual. This usually indicates sadness and fatigue. But it could also connote pent-up anger or frustration.

You can easily pinpoint people's real intentions by looking at their paralanguage and their body language as a whole. If you see that there is a disconnect between their pitch, their verbal message, and their body language, you can infer that something's wrong or that person is hiding something from you.

Volume

This refers to the loudness or softness of one's voice at any given time. If you're speaking in front of people at a distance you may need to project your voice louder. But if you are speaking with a person individually, you may want to soften your voice. When you are trying to find the appropriate volume in a specific event, consider two things:

1. Is what you're saying confidential? Will it make someone uncomfortable? Is it unnecessary for others to know? If the answer is yes, it is important to speak quietly. If possible, talk with that person in a quieter and more secluded place such as the corner of a lobby or a conference room. The other person will surely appreciate your approach in dealing with sensitive topics such as financial information.
2. The next thing to consider is how the person will speak back to you. Do they have a booming voice? Are they likely to

ask for clarification? Do they have hearing problems? If so, it is important to speak up to match the volume needs of your client. However, you also need to make sure that you don't escalate your voice so much that your client receives it as a display of anger or frustration.

When you're assessing someone's posture, it is important to learn about the forms and kinds of posture for a clearer interpretation. Matched with your knowledge in proxemics, you will better see the positioning of other people's bodies and determine what they convey. In learning this information, not only can you assess other's true intentions, but you can also improve your posture and your ability to convey information using body language and paralanguage. In the next chapter, we will discuss more about positive and negative body language so you can assess how often you do it. Learning these will also help you read people's body language as a whole to determine if they are genuine or if they have hidden intentions.

Chapter 5 – Positive versus Negative

How Often Do You Show Positive and Negative Body Language?

In the previous chapters, we have discussed dynamic and static posture as well as closed and open posture. We identified closed posture as a person's way of protecting themselves from unwanted emotions such as fear, anger, frustration, sadness, or anxiety. Open posture, on the other hand, refers to a more positive outlook of the environment. This is characterized by one's readiness to take on another day. It is also characterized by one's willingness to learn, interest, excitement, and joy.

Before you get to assess the body language of other people, you need to understand positive and negative body language. If you understand it, you will have a better baseline of appropriate interaction strategies. You will also learn how to pinpoint disconnects in people's body language, which is essential if you want to reveal one's true intentions.

In this chapter, we will discuss positive and negative body language which is essential in reading people's intent and meaning.

Positive Body Language

Positive body language is often regarded as appealing, receptive, and approachable. It gives people a sense of comfort, dignity, and likability. Aside from these, it makes others open in interacting with people this is why it is important to display this type of body language to build rapport and trust with other people.

If you want to show positive body language, remember that you should not show defensiveness. Defensive body language usually discourages people from approaching you making it more difficult to build a relationship. It is also important not to display a sense of disinterest towards other people because it can lead to disconnect which will bode ill if you're planning to land a job or plan to convince more partners.

Another key factor in showing positive body language is having a neutral stance. You should not show authority nor submissiveness. But at the same time, you need to be able to assert or put forth your opinions confidently without giving offense to other people. Here are some strategies on how you can show positive body language.

1. Stand erect. The first rule in displaying positive body language is to stand straight. Your back must be erect, so you give the impression of being tall. According to psychology, a taller appearance usually connotes a good impression as compared to slouching or hunching.

   When you slouch, you give your audience the impression that you're lazy and that you are irresponsible. It also shows that you have a very passive personality and that you have low self-esteem.

2. The second rule you need to consider if you want to show positive body language is to face the person you're talking to. Do not face sideways, and most importantly, do not turn your back from the person you're talking to. When you stand sideways, it shows that you want to run from that person and that you want to discontinue the interaction. Conversely, you need to observe if the other person does this. This means that he or she is uninterested in what you're offering.

   According to experts, the best way to interact with your clients is to direct your heart towards the other person. This means that your heart is facing the heart of your client without any obstruction in between. I guess it's safe to say that you're speaking heart to heart. During this process, avoid crossing your arms over your chest. This is a big NO in the corporate world, especially when you're trying to land a job or trying to seal a deal. This is one of the most common turnoffs.

3. The third most important goal is to free your hands. Most people like to hide their hands in their pockets while they're talking to people. This is another big NO. It usually means that you're not confident about what you're offering or that you are withholding some information that could be suspicious to your clients. As much as possible, show your hands and use them to emphasize your points. This way, you can convey trust and reliability to the other party.

4. Another rule in the business world is to look people in the eyes. However, you need to determine the limit of the average time of gazing. On average, you can make direct eye contact for two to three seconds while conveying a point then break away from time to time. This will keep you from intimidating your client.

5. The last but not the least way to show positive body language is to move and show some limb movements. When you show that your extremities are too stiff, it could indicate that you are anxious or that you lack confidence. It could also mean that you are withholding information from the other party. So, from time to time, switch the position of your leg but as much as possible do not cross it so they don't get the impression that you are closed about their ideas.

Positive body language is not only important when building intimate relationships. It is also important in the workplace where people are trying to make deals and to convince clients to avail products and services.

Negative Body Language

If there is positive body language, there is also a negative counterpart. In this segment, we will discuss what negative body language is and how it shows from the people you interact with. Conversely, we will tackle some of the most common negative body languages you may be doing that can turn people off.

Negative body language expresses undesirable feelings through gestures, facial expressions, and paralanguage. It could be conscious or unconscious expressions that show what a person feels during an event.

Some of the most common negative body languages you can observe from people include folded arms and crossed legs. Both could indicate that they are not paying attention or that they are close-minded about your opinions. Another common body language is turning their head or body away from you. This could mean that they are uninterested, or they feel angry or frustrated towards you. Another thing you can observe from people with negative feelings is a lack of eye contact or looking down. It could mean that they are not truthful, shy, or afraid of you.

During public interactions, you can spot negative body language that expresses people's feelings. When your audience is bored, you can see them slouching, looking at their watches or phones, fidgeting, and fiddling with items. If you observe your audience with these body languages, it's time to check yourself. Maybe you're not coming off as commanding and interesting to your audience. It's also possible that you are embodying negative body language.

Here are some of the common body language mistakes that disconnect speakers from their audience:

1. **Lack of eye contact**.
   This tells your audience that your mind is elsewhere, that you are not present in the moment. If they see this, they too will divert their attention to something else. Remember that when you are speaking in public, you command the audience. Chances are that people will mirror what they see. So, if you make them see that you are inattentive while speaking, they will also lose their focus.

2. **Staring at your phone or your notes often.**
   This makes the audience feel that you are not confident with your speech. It even makes it seem like you doubt what you say, which makes the audience question your position to discuss specific topics.

3. **Talking too fast.**
   Another negative body language is talking too fast. This exudes nervousness and self-doubt that causes a disconnect between you and the audience. Remember that people have different ways of processing information. Some process it quickly, while some people need more time to digest ideas. So, you have to deliver your speech at an average rate, which according to the National Center for Voice and Speech, is

around 150 words per minute. As the speaker, it is your responsibility to allow your audience to take in what you are saying. So, relax, breathe, and take your time so your audience can listen and understand your points.

4. **Using too many filler words.**
Filler words such as "ah," "Uhm," "like," and many more are signs of nervousness and self-doubt. If you use too many of these filler words, it could mean that you are not prepared and that you are doubting what you are about to say. This can easily turn your audience off.

5. **Too much use of negative language**.
During public speaking, one of the best turn-offs is using too much negative language. Especially when talking about sensitive subjects like gender, beliefs, religion, medicine, and psychology, it's best to approach topics lightly. Take a look at these examples,

"Stop believing in fairytales. It will not get you anywhere."
"You will not succeed if you keep doing this."
"If you are narcissistic, you are cunning and manipulative."

As you can see, there is too much use of negative language. If you hear people say this to you, will you not feel a bit offended or attacked? Especially when you have the same thinking, these statements will make you feel apprehended or upset. Instead of this approach, you can reword your statements to sound more positive.

"While fairytales give us hope that there is a happy ever after in every story, we still need to think realistically about our goals."
"There is a greater chance of succeeding if you adopt this approach."
"People with narcissism are usually cunning and manipulative."

6. Closed posture

We discussed in the previous chapter what a closed posture is. While it can give you comfort and protection from unwanted thoughts, you should control when to embody it. When you show a closed posture in front of an audience, they might think that you have low confidence. This leads them to believe that you are unreliable. So, as much as possible, be aware of your actions when you're speaking in public always portray a positive posture to your audience.

7. Folding arms

While speaking with other people, especially when there's a table to rest their arms on, people tend to cross their arms. This might be a way to relax your limbs and show that you are paying attention. But understand that people interpret events and actions in different ways. You may come off as uninterested or closed from their opinions which could affect your transaction. So, it's essential to free your hands and use them to emphasize your thoughts. If you're not speaking, you still need to show your hands and maintain an open position. This will help your client see that you are open to their opinions.

8. Scrunched face

Ever heard the term "resting bitch face"? It's where people look naturally fierce and intimidating, which can be off-putting, especially in social interactions. Most people are not aware that they have a resting bitch face which affects how they interact with others. It makes the audience fear you instead of approach you. It also makes them feel intimidated by you, which could make your presentation ineffective and uninteresting.

If you suspect you have this look, record yourself while speaking. This way, you will see if you show a scrunched or frowning face while presenting. If so, practice smiling more and showing diverse facial expressions that match your opinions. This way, you can emphasize your point and show your audience that you are approachable. And remember, if you want to convince people and seal deals, your default facial expression should be a smile.

9. **Being too stiff**

The next negative body language that can break deals is being too stiff. This usually happens when a person is shy or anxious. If a speaker is too stiff, all other movements can seem like awkward twitches. It makes the audience doubt your ability to command the crowd, and so, they might take your presentation for granted.

One of the techniques to keep this from happening is to loosen up before you go and stage. You might have seen performers shake their bodies before the event? You can do this too, if you want to calm your nerves. You can also do mindful breathing. This process helps you clear your mind from unwanted thoughts. It also allows you to convince your mind that there's nothing to be afraid of. With practice, you can manipulate your brain to let go of that nervousness and go all-in when presenting in front of an audience. You'll be surprised how impactful these techniques are in exuding confidence and captivating the crowd.

10. Lack of dynamism while speaking

The last but not the least form of negative body language is having a stagnant presentation. Either one is standing so still rather than moving around and engaging the crowd, or one is speaking in a monotonous tone. Whatever the case is, it shows the audience that a person is not confident.

To keep this from happening, it is important to own the stage as discussed in the previous chapters. When it comes to your voice, apply some dynamism to it. Instead of speaking to your audience in one note, add variations to your tone.

Imagine a person saying, "I've got exciting news!" in a monotonous voice. Hearing this, it's almost impossible to believe that the speaker will deliver good news. Chances are, you don't want to listen to what he or she is about to say. But if you hear them add flair to the words by adding quirkiness or eccentricity, you will feel their excitement, and you will feel eager to listen.

These negative body languages are very common. So, it is important to check yourself and determine which negative body language you use. Record yourself while you practice and tally how many times you show negative gestures and facial expressions. After which, you know better to be aware of your actions whenever you're interacting with people.

Aside from determining whether people are bored or inattentive, you can also use negative body language to assess when one is lying. In the next chapter, let's discuss one of the most controversial issues in society—lying and deception. Is lying always intentional? How do you determine when a person is truthful or not? Let's find out!

Chapter 6 – Liar, Liar, Pants on Fire

Why do we lie? Is it always intentional?

Almost everyone has   lied at one point in their lives, be it intentionally or unintentionally. Sometimes, it's a spur-of-the-moment decision out of panic or urgency. Whatever the case is, nobody   can deny that   lying and deception are not a   decent practice. Unfortunately, people have become so good at lying that they don't feel guilty anymore or they neglect to think about the problems and catastrophes it can create. Sure, you may have gained something from   deceiving   others   like   discounts, promotions, sales, or commission. But at the end of the day, there is damage being inflicted on the system.

When we say system, it affects all the facets that an event or a scenario encompasses. It includes the one being lied to, the liar, the environment, and probably everyone who is involved in a specific case.

Let's take this scenario. In XYZ Company, three people are up for a promotion. During their interviews, person A and B were honest about their contributions to the company. In contrast, person C took the liberty of adding and editing their performance in the past year. This made the manager choose employee C over A and B. While this is beneficial for the employee, it affected the career, self-esteem, and probably even the personal lives of employee A and B. The company will also suffer from this lie because their new assistant director could not deliver the results expected from them. This could lead to bankruptcy or low productivity. As a result, employee C will either get fired or be demoted.

So, you see, even if you get the most out of a lie, there will always be a consequence waiting to happen. This leaves the question, is lying always intentional?

Most people agree that lying is intentional wherein people are fully aware of their actions. This is why most victims of lying feel frustrated, deceived, and angry at people who lied or withheld the truth. Often, when they spot an excessive liar, they immediately cut their ties out of fear or annoyance. Little do they know that lying can be automatic to some people, especially those with psychological disorders. Although this does not make lying acceptable, it gives you a deeper understanding as to why they lie. It also allows you to alleviate your feelings of frustration and anger and it will help you heal and move on.

Research has proven that humans have the innate need to protect themselves from unwanted feelings and events. In spur-of-the-moment decisions, people tend to choose their self-interest without considering the consequences. This happens when people panic. Even if it's not their intention to lie, somehow, they manage to withhold the truth for self-preservation. This is usually observed among children who grew up in a hostile environment. Because they already know the consequences of their actions, their immediate response is denial when they are being accused. The same is true among adults. Research has proven that people lie without deliberating about the consequences as long as the lie contributes to their self-interest. For example, during job interviews, the human resource personnel can ask if a person is willing to work long hours. Because most are taught to say yes with whatever job requirement, the initial response to any of their questions is "yes" even if the applicant does not really want to travel as much. In his or her mind, the initial goal is to land the job and they'll figure it out from there. So, it's possible that employee C from the previous example lied automatically to land the promotion because of their needs.

Another possible reason why people lie is the fact that memories can change over time as a product of new learning. Sometimes, the thoughts and memories in our brains assimilate with one another, forming a new story that the mind believes is the truth. So, even if the person does not intend to lie, there is an inconsistency in their stories because of "retrieval-enhanced suggestibility."

In research conducted, participants watched a film then they were asked to come back for a memory test a few days later. In between watching the movie and the memory test, other events happened. Half of the participants were given a practice memory test while the other half were given a description of the film to read which included some incorrect details.

Come the memory test, the researchers found that people added the false details to their description of the movie. You'll be surprised that the people who took the practice test reproduced the false information more than those who read an incorrect description. In this study, the researchers have inferred that when it comes to memory, practice makes imperfect. This is proven by another theory that rehearsing memories can make them more malleable. It is likened to taking the ice cream out from the freezer and putting it under the sun. By the time the ice cream goes back to the freezer, it would have become misshapen. It's probably one of the reasons why people lie unintentionally, it is a result of the malleability of memories.

The last but not the least reason why lying can be automatic is habit. There are instances when people have lied so many times that it has become their second nature. Although they do not have psychological disorders, lying is just inherent to them, which makes them lie even when they don't need to.   If you know someone who lies a lot, this is probably caused by the Pinocchio problem.

You all know the story of Pinocchio, written by Italian author Carlo Collodi. In the story portrayed by Disney, Pinocchio was carved by a woodcarver named Gepetto in a Tuscan village. Pinocchio was created as a puppet, but he dreamed of becoming a real boy. However, he is known for his frequent tendency to lie. And it's not because of any psychological disorder. He just likes to lie without any apparent reason. So, psychologists coined the Pinocchio problem to describe people who lied a lot but do not fit the criteria of becoming pathological, sociopathic, or compulsive liars. What is the reason people have this problem? Here are some of the most common reasons why:

Fear

Tad Williams, an American fantasy and science fiction writer, said that people tell lies when they're afraid. It could be what other people might think or do when they find out the truth. Many people believe that when they tell a lie, fear is alleviated but it only gets stronger because then people know the need to keep up with the lie. And often, they're afraid that people might find out the truth from others which will only worsen the situation.

This reason for lying is commonly observed in people who have experienced abuse. When a child grows up in a physically or emotionally abusive household, they are afraid to speak up. They're afraid to be honest because they already know the consequences. Unfortunately, some people carry this behavior outside a household and lie to other people as well even if the consequences are not as fearful as they anticipated it to be.

Manipulation

Another reason why people lie is the desire to manipulate the situation. Either people want to get away with negative behavior, or they want to get something out of people like sex, status, money, power, love, and many more. Unfortunately, the most common approach that people do to get what they want is saying the words, "I love you." This eight-letter sentence could be the most wonderful to hear, or it could also be the most dangerous. You never know if the people closest to you are lying and manipulating you until you find out the truth. This is why it is important to protect yourself by learning more.

Lying to manipulate also happens when people feel like they're losing control. They often lie to control people and situations around them to regain a sense of control and somehow alleviate their anxiety.

If you're a victim of manipulation and emotional abuse, you can break free from those harmful relationships and redevelop healthy connections that affirm your sense of worth. Part of the resolution is to identify if you are manipulated. You either call them out or cut the relationship completely. It all helps by talking to a therapist, confiding in a friend, and spending time in places and communities that nourish you are great first steps.

Shame

This is one of the most common reasons for lying. When people do something wrong and they are embarrassed by it, they tend to make up stories to cover what they did. They either blame it on someone else or they deny the reason and put others in front of the bus. One example of this is making stories to hide the shame of damaging intimate relationships by cheating. The downside is instead of coming clean and rebuilding the relationship, they hide the behavior until their partner finds out through slips of the tongue, uncovered tracks, and gossip. This will further ruin the relationship, and it could make it unfixable.

Hiding Addiction

A person who has an addictive behavior feels both fear and shame. This is the result of the standards and laws in society. An example is drug addiction. Because it is illegal in countries, people lie about it to their friends and family. At first, it's all fun and games. Still, when the addiction gets a hold of your psyche, it could lead to a dysfunctional life affecting your relationships, career, and overall productivity.

Another example is alcohol addiction. People pay less attention to drinking as a form of addiction, but it is as harmful as drug addiction. In no time, people will prioritize drinking over other priorities, which could lead to lying and deception. You can only imagine the lengths that people go through just to get a sip of alcohol.

Pride

Another common reason for lying is to boost one's pride and self-confidence. It could be in the form of exaggerating your accomplishments or minimizing the threats and problems—any approach that makes them look better to other people. They want to feel the grandiosity and superiority among people because they want to be adored and complimented.

In some cases, this type of lying seems harmless. But like alcohol and drugs, the feeling of grandiosity and superiority are addictive. If this happens, people could develop narcissistic personality disorder. This is characterized by an exaggerated sense of superiority and an uncontrollable preoccupation with success and power.

These are only some of the most common reasons why people lie. And as you can see, it is not as uncommon as you think. It's actually pretty typical because people are constantly protecting their egos from unwanted thoughts and pain.

In fact, in a study conducted by Robert Feldman in 2002 at the University of Massachusetts Amherst, he found that 60% of people lied during a 10-minute conversation. And in that span, the participants told an average of two to three lies. Suppose people can lie in a controlled environment. What can stop them from lying in their natural environment where they can say whatever they want?

A forensic psychologist at the Haas School of Business at the University of California, Dr. Leanne ten Brinke noted that people have good instincts in detecting lies. Still, our conscious minds usually fail us by seeing facts first before gut-feels. This is why people have moments when they say, "I knew it! He was lying!"

At the moment, the conscious mind only processed what the person was doing and how they acted. Even when the subconscious screamed, "He's a manipulator," the conscious mind battled this notion and said, "We have no facts to prove that." This is why people are easily manipulated and lied to and it stops now. You cannot control people and you cannot stop them from lying. What you can do is equip yourself with the knowledge you need to determine whether or not a person is lying to you. This will serve as your protection from unwanted advances and circumstances in relation to lying and deception.

Dr. Lillian Glass, a behavioral analyst, body language expert, and author of "The Body Language of Liars" worked with the FBI. She imposed that one should understand how people react in specific situations to catch a liar. Along with her techniques in observing facial reactions and emotions, body language, and speech patterns. Let's take a look at the seven interesting ways to spot a liar.

7 Ways to Spot a Liar

Before we discuss the signs of lying, it is crucial to establish a baseline, as we have discussed in the previous chapters. This is necessary to create a more accurate assumption in determining the possibility of someone lying. So, without further ado, here are seven signs you need to watch out for to figure out if someone is lying.

1. They change their head position quickly.

According to FBI agents, this is one of the most common signs that a person is not being truthful. The idea behind this is, when someone is scared, nervous, or hiding something, their body intensifies and stiffens because they're trying to prevent any unwanted body language that can throw them off.

So, when they're asked the question, they change their head position quickly. They either bow or tilt their head to the side. And if this happens, you can observe a jerkiness to their movements. When someone is relaxed, even if they move, you can see a natural and smooth movement. But when

146

someone is nervous and possibly lying, there is a stiffness in their actions that can give them away.

2. Their breathing may also change.

Someone's breathing may become heavier when lying. It's a reflex that comes along with the increase of heart rate. You can observe this through the sound of their breathing or when their shoulders rise, and their voice gets shallow.

3. They don't blink.

This is a tough sign to spot, especially without knowledge about body language. As we discussed in the previous chapters, liars have perfected their confidence when interacting with other people. Because of this, they have learned not to break eye contact even if they are lying. Instead, they will stare at their interrogator to make them seem genuine. But if you look closely, you can observe that there is a decreased rate of blinking. It means that they can control their eye movements, to the point that they are disrupting the natural reflex of their eyes to blink. This gives you a clue that they might not be telling the truth.

In contrast, some liars usually have an increased blinking rate which could indicate that they are nervous, or they are withholding something. This is why it is important to create a baseline before interrogating someone. This way, you can determine when their thinking rate decreases or increases when you ask a question.

4. **They pause before answering.**
This refers to a long pause before someone answers a question. It means that people are either thinking about an alternative answer or simply withholding the truth. Sometimes, people forgot what they said moments before, and they're trying to remember it, so their next statement matches. You can observe this in their gestures and facial expressions.

5. **They touch their face, mouth, or throat**.

Another common sign that a person is lying is touching vulnerable parts of their body such as their face, mouth, abdomen, chest, neck, or head. According to psychologists, this form of behavior is a way of shielding the mind from unwanted stimuli. A person automatically does this when he or she does not want to deal with an issue or answer a question. Instead of explaining, they are closing off communication by covering specific body parts.

When the hands touch the throat for example, it could mean that they have an increased rate of swallowing, which is another sign of lying. When the hands cover the eyes, it could mean that they have increased blinking or that they are looking down.

6. They provide too much information.

There is a very high probability that a person is not telling you the truth when someone rambles on, giving too much information. Even when specific information is not requested, they tell it anyway, possibly because of nervousness. In a liars' mind, when they give too much information, they can make people believe that what they are saying is true. By giving the whole story, they think that the people surrounding them will no longer ask questions because every piece of information they need to know is already in their made-up story.

This is also a strategy to derail and distract the interrogator from his or her trail of questions. Instead of focusing on the main issue, the interrogator will then delve into the pertinent details. But then again, if you're a skilled interrogator and an active listener, you can see that some of the information does not match. There is incoherence. Plus, most of what has been said is not related to the main topic or issue. It's your responsibility to funnel the important details and ask them more about it. Don't hesitate to cut them off and ask follow-up questions because this can derail them from their train of thought.

7. **They tend to resort to hostility and defensiveness**

The last but not the least sign of lying is hostility and defensiveness. And with good reason! Most liars resort to negative behavior by raising their voices and exaggerating their movements to hide the fact that they are nervous. They tend to turn the situation around to make the interrogator feel like they are a bad person for accusing an innocent person. Often, you can hear them say that they are respected by the community and that they have a couple of accomplishments. But if you think of it, what does this information have to do with the main issue? This gives you a red flag that the person you're talking to might be lying.

Another strategy that people do when they lie is they blame other people for the situation. And when you ask more about it, you can see that they know more about the issue even if you haven't given any information yet. Out of the nervousness they feel, they are already telling pieces of the truth but putting someone else's name on the line. It's a classic move and unfortunately, many people fall for it.

Identifying the Kind of Liar You are Facing

Lying is such a controversial topic in society. When you ask people around you if lying is wrong and if they are likely to do it, you'll be surprised about their responses. Most people will say that lying is good or bad, depending on the situation. And if you ask them if they are likely to do it, many will say yes. This is proven by Dr. Feldman, author of the most recent Journal of Basic and Applied Social Psychology. In his studies, he found that 60% of people lie every day and the average is around two to three lies. This is backed by a study conducted by DePaulo and his colleagues about Lying in Everyday Life. They interviewed a number of college students and community members. During the process, 77 students admitted to telling an average of two lies a day. In addition, 70 community members told the researchers that they lie at least once a day.

This leaves the question, "What types of lies do people tell every day?" and "Are all liars the same?"

According to research, the type of lie people tell depends on the kind of liar they are. Did you know that there are five types of liars? Let's discuss them one by one.

Pathological liar

This is a person who lies incessantly to get what they want with little awareness. Because they have been lying for so long, lying has become their nature. These people may not even be conscious that they just told a lie. This is viewed by experts as a coping mechanism developed in early childhood. And usually, it is associated with mental health disorders like antisocial personality disorder. It's possible that these people have become so good at lying because they're protecting themselves from traumatic experiences such as abuse. Chances are, they will continue to lie to protect themselves from harm.

Pathological liars are usually goal-oriented. They lie to get what they want, often to exaggerate their worth. When they talk about their accomplishments, they make it seem like they are heroes, the people wouldn't have survived without them. But if they fail or they do something embarrassing, they play the victim to gain sympathy and acceptance from others. As a skilled lie detector, you can easily observe when one is a pathological liar when their stories are overly dramatic and complicated. They make their stories seem so detailed and colorful in hopes to make people adore them. Plus, they exude this confidence using their body language as a conduit for people to believe that they are telling the truth.

The worst part about pathological liars is their lies have become their truth. This is why they have a weaker grip on reality. If people attempt to make them realize what is real, it is enough to cause breakdown and hostility.

Compulsive Liar

This is different from being a compulsive liar. These are people who lie is out of habit. Compulsive liars tell lies even when they don't have to, and they bend the truth about everything. According to psychologists, compulsive lying is a common behavior that develops in early childhood due to being raised in an environment where lying is necessary and routine. Many of these people find it difficult to manage confrontations and tackle consequences head-on. Hence, they resort to lying. This behavior is usually observed in people who have attention-deficit/hyperactivity disorder (ADHD), bipolar disorder, and borderline personality disorder.

The difference between compulsive liars and pathological liars is that the former is not manipulative. They just lie out of habit. It just became an automatic response that is very difficult to break. In addition, their lies are easier to point out because their stories usually do not add up. Plus, they're very obvious in displaying lying behaviors such as avoiding eye contact, sweating, stuttering, or rambling. They also lie out of spite, even if they don't necessarily get anything from it. And when you confront them, they're more likely to admit to lying, but this does not stop them from telling more lies.

Does this mean that if someone lies a lot, they are considered a pathological or compulsive liar? Note that people need to be assessed by professionals for them to classify into these disorders. So, be careful when making assumptions about people who lie a lot. They need to meet specific criteria before they are considered pathological or compulsive liars. Although these are formally included in the Diagnostic and Statistical Manual of Mental Disorders, psychologists can recognize these behaviors as a sign of an underlying psychological disorder.

Sociopathic liar

These types of liars are very difficult to deal with because they lack empathy. They don't care if their lies cause harm to people and their careers, relationships, and health. This is probably the reason why they're called the most dangerous liars. They can make you doubt yourself and question your morals. And they will not even feel guilt for the harm they caused. These people like to play mind games to control everyone in their environment including their loved ones. And because they're charming, most people believe their lies and are likely to give them what they want.

Compared to compulsive and pathological liars, sociopathic liars do not respect the law or the norms. They can use false identities and nicknames to get what they want. Plus, they consistently display aggressive or aggravated behavior especially when they're called out. They are known for lashing out at people trying to help them or for calling out their behaviors.

White Liars

Next are white liars. These people often mix the truth with lies either to protect themselves or to avoid insulting and hurting other people. White lies could be in the form of making excuses. For example, a person you don't like is asking you to attend their birthday party. Instead of saying, "No, thanks because I don't like you," you often come up with a reason why you can't come. This is a more polite way to turn people down and avoid hurting their feelings.

White lies also arise when people attempt to hide parts of the truth because they believe that this will hurt other people. A very common example is when somebody asks if their dish is delicious. Of course, even if you didn't like it, you will pretend that you did so the chef will not get hurt.

Another reason why people tell white lies is to protect themselves from confrontation. This usually happens in job interviews, particularly when the human resource personnel asks why people left their old jobs. Some people would emphasize the negative factors that affected their work and productivity and leave out that they were fired because of their offenses.

Many people believe that this type of lie is harmless. To the liars maybe, but it can be detrimental to other people. The chef's dish, for example, what if they served the same dish to more critical people? The chef could receive insults that could lower his self-esteem and lead to then feeling demotivated in pursuing their career. Had you been more honest in the beginning, they could have improved the dish to get more praise from other customers.

This is why lying is controversial. Most people often experience a dilemma between telling the truth or hurting other's feelings. In this case, it's probably better to always tell the truth even when it hurts. When people believe that you're honest, you can establish trust and reliability. It will help you build relationships with the people close to you.

Another reason why truthfulness is important is you don't have to bear the guilt of withholding information. You know what they say, "The truth shall set you free." It can also help you keep your sanity. Even if you cannot control the reaction of other people, you can keep a clean conscience and you can let go and heal from the situation.

Occasional liars

The last but not the least category of liars is occasional liars. You cannot deny that most people lie occasionally for various reasons. Still, this should not be applauded or accepted. These statements, whether big or small can still cause an impact on the environment and the people in it. Although these people seldomly lie, many believe them because they are so used to hearing the truth. And when these people lie, they don't know if the statement is correct or not.

The upside is, once you study their body language and create a baseline, you can determine when they are lying. If you suspect so, there's no harm in confronting them because these people will usually feel guilty and will admit to their lies. If you call out an occasional liar, chances are, they will feel genuinely sorry and will work on their behavior.

Those Who Lie Behind the Safety of a Screen

If you think liars can only present themselves personally, some liars exist behind the safety of a screen. This means that they lie through various blogs, news, online applications, and social media platforms like Facebook, Twitter, Instagram, and many more.

Browsing through these platforms, you can see interesting information from news, blogs, and stories. Unfortunately, only a few of them are factual and correct. In most cases, even if the headline is correct, the article consists of fabrications and hear-say. Other times, people omit important information to make one party look worse than the other. This is more common in politics. Fans and advocates of each party write news and articles that exaggerate the accomplishments of a candidate. During debates and issues, they highlight the positive information about that person and neglect adding what they did wrong. The worst part is media platforms use the strength of their network to show credibility. This is why millions of people are deceived.

Other forms of deception that liars use are e-mails and chats. These are evident in mailing applications, dating platforms, and social media. Often, scammers use these tools to engage their victims and get them to disclose enough information to use their names to initiate a scam. Here are some of the most common types of scams you need to watch out for:

1. **Advance fee fraud**

   Advance fee fraud. This is the process in which scammers request fees or information upfront in exchange for goods, services, money, or rewards. But upon payment, the scammers will cut all forms of interaction, leaving the victims at a loss. The most common victims of advance fee fraud are people who are new to the internet. Sometimes, because they lack guidance, they seek help from any person on the web. Some are also easily captivated by discounts and freebies. Little do they know that these people are about to take their money.

2. **Sweepstakes and competition scams**

   This is another technique that scammers use to get money from victims. Scammers will communicate with you via chat or email claiming to be agents of sweepstakes and lottery companies.

They will say that you have won fantastic prizes like a house lot, money, or car. But before you claim them, you need to give money upfront for "delivery fees" or "service fees." So unless you did join the lottery or any raffle, be wary when interacting with people who claim that you've won a prize.

3. Dating and romance scams

This next form of scam is no longer new to people. These scams occur when scammers create fake profiles on legitimate dating websites. They can use other people's names and identity to get you to believe that they're legit. Then, they will try to build a relationship with you so they can siphon money using "love" or "affection."

They will tell stories, making you believe that they badly need the money. These scammers can tell you that they or their family member is sick, that they need to travel, or they need to pay for tuition. Chances are, because they already got you to fall for them, you will not hesitate to give them money. After this, either these people will give "proof" of their expenditures to you so they can exploit more resources. It's also possible that upon payment, these people will permanently cut their ties. Note how cunning and patient these people are. They will spend months, even years, to convince you. They will take time to earn your trust. That's when they will hit jackpot.

4. Computer Hacking

Many scammers will attempt to access your computer and gather as much information about you. This includes your name, address, passwords, bank account numbers, even ID numbers.

Why do criminals want to access your personal information? It's simple. They want to sell your personal data to criminals so they can use it on the dark web. Once they get access to your most pertinent details, you are now subject to identity theft. They can use your profile to avail credit cards and loans and will spend this money however they want. In the end, your name is at stake answering to the expenses they made.

Another reason why scammers want your personal information is they want to frame you for their acts. Aside from stealing, they can initiate other crimes and make you liable for them. They can take control of your social media account and emails to commit more scams and extortions. It can be used for spying and manipulation.

It's also possible that they want to harm companies. They can wipe out your data or falsify your documents which can be detrimental to people and their companies.

To achieve this, most scammers use phishing through social media and email. They will trick you to open links or attachments. When you do, a malicious software will be installed on your device and the hacker will gather as much data as they can.

5. **Auction shopping and online shopping**

Many scammers use legitimate selling platforms to scam people. Typically, they offer several products and they will convince you to avail them. But before they deliver, they will require you to give money upfront or to key in your bank account details, usually outside the selling platform. When they get what they want, they either deliver an inferior item, a faulty item, or nothing at all. This is what online sellers call nowadays bogus sellers.

6. Banking and credit card scams

One strategy where scammers can exploit money from you is hacking your bank account. Typically, they will send you an e-mail or text, saying that there are anomalies in your bank account. They can even call you, pretending to be professionals and agents of your bank. These scammers will make you feel the urgency of the situation. And to fix this, you will need to disclose your name, phone number, and bank details for "verification." When they get enough information, it is enough to duplicate copies of your ATM card and exploit your account.

Another way that scammers can get your bank details is by putting a discreet attachment like cameras to ATMs or EFTPOS machines. This way, they can capture your account details, including your pin and CVV. When this happens, they can use your account for online purchases and other transactions.

7. Small business scams

Next on the list is using small business scams to extort money from people using small businesses. Scammers usually issue fake listings and products for free to trick you into signing up. Little do you know that there is a hidden subscription in the fine print. You may not be paying for the main product, but they will make you pay for the other items associated with the "free" product.

An example of this is scammers offering an application for free. But once you avail, they will get you to pay for monthly serial codes.

Another modus that scammers use is pretending to be small business owners. They will entice you to sign up to their website for free to enjoy freebies, updates, and prizes. Some will even initiate raffles just to get you to disclose your personal information. When you do, they will claim that you ordered products from them and they will make you pay for it. If you hesitate, they will threaten to sue you or report you to the authorities. This is why many people are scammed by these people.

8. Employment scams

This scam is very common among third world and developing countries because scammers will disguise themselves as employment agents. Seeing the difficulty of landing a job in some areas, many people are desperate in trusting these opportunities. These scammers will offer a job with a high salary. They even promise opportunities to work overseas on one condition. You need to give upfront payments for training, software, uniforms, service fees, clearances, and many more.

Be wary of these scams as they can present themselves legally and enticingly.

9. Gambling scams

This is much like small business scams, but they offer investment in real estate stocks, or foreign currency trading. Some will even offer lottery tickets, betting in horse races, and other sports events. They will claim to be professionals who can handle your investments strategically. But once you give them your money, you'll soon find that the people or the company does not exist at all.

10. Charity scams

Charity or medical scams are the most common on social media because it is the easiest way to convince people. The scammers will make up stories that they or their families are sick, and they need medical assistance. Other times, they can use other people's identities, real sick people and collect money for a cause. At the end of the day, the ill do not receive the donations but the scammers.

Lying online has become easier, don't you think? Especially with the lack of guidance, people can fall for these tricks easily. This is why it is important to learn when to trust people and how to detect online liars.

According to law enforcers, there are signs when scammers are trying to phish personal information to commit fraud or theft. Be vigilant when you observe the following signs:

Scammers will attempt to communicate with you with a sense of urgency, especially when committing bank theft, identity theft, or small business scams. You will receive an e-mail or a text. Some even receive phone calls out of the blue. They will ask your name and address, along with your bank account number to verify your information. Usually, these messages are poorly written, or they contain grammatical errors. Often, they also do not use the correct symbols and format as formal companies would use. Some of the main headlines or content they use include:

"Your mailbox has been hacked!"

"Your Facebook account has been compromised!"

"There have been unusual transactions using your account. Verify it's you."

Some victims also reported to receive pop-ups on their phones or computers, asking if they wanted to allow a specific software to run. If you receive these notifications but did not download any new application, you need to be wary.

How do you know if your accounts have already been compromised? First, you're unable to log into your accounts or someone logged in from an unusual location. You will notice unusual conversations or activities in your account. Your money will also go missing from your bank account. Often, your credit card will reach its limit, so it keeps getting declined.

Another sign of being compromised is financial institutions refuse to give you service because your credit score is low or because you already have a criminal record. In turn, you will receive bills and invoices for goods or services you didn't purchase. People will also start contacting you because they believe that they have been dealing with you. But in reality, someone has been using your identity to interact with them.

Seeing how dangerous and verifying scams are, it is important to protect yourself. As much as possible, do not pull them suspicious emails or texts, even when they have a sense of urgency. Delete these immediately to keep yourself safe.

When someone calls and they claim to be representatives of your bank account, do not disclose any personal information. Some will even pretend to be friends with your family members. They will make up a story saying that your brother, sister, spouse, or parent is in the hospital and in dire need of financial help. Before you believe any of these calls, verify it with the specific people or company.

It's also important to decline whenever you're being asked to download a suspicious file or to click on a suspicious link. Delete these immediately to prevent scammers from hacking your devices.

Another important way to protect yourself against scams is to choose strong passwords. Many people take this precautionary measure for granted. They usually claim that they have no money to offer anyway, so why make their passwords difficult to remember? In most cases, hackers who want to commit identity theft will choose accounts with the easiest passwords. So, even if you don't have money to offer, they can steal your identity and use it to commit fraud.

Law enforcement agencies warn people never to use names or birthdays as passwords. It's also important to mix complex characters such as capital letters and numbers. This way, it almost impossible to guess.

Another technique to prevent scams and hacks is to secure your networks and devices with reliable antivirus and firewall software. As much as possible, do not connect to public servers or Wi-Fi hot spots when trying to access personal information such as bank details.

How to Assess Lies in Texts and E-mails

According to a recent study, workers receive an average of 121 emails a day. With this number, some emails are phishing strategies while others contain fake news.

Hackers and scammers are cunning and highly deceiving. So, even if they appear to be legitimate companies and professionals in texts or emails, you still need to be vigilant before clicking on any links or disclosing any information. Luckily, there are signs that can give you clues as to when a person is being truthful or not. In a recent study performed in Austin, Texas, the researchers found that it is possible to predict lies based on phrases and sentence constructions. How? Here are major red flags:

1. Lack of first-person pronouns

When people are being truthful, chances are they will use first-person pronouns such as I, me, we, and us. One way you can assess when an e-mail or a text is a scam is too much use of second-person pronouns like 'you,' and third-person pronouns such as him, her, it, they, and many more. Researchers have proven that this is a common pattern across chronic liars. In their studies, they ran e-mails filled with lies on a lie-detecting software program. And they found out that 67% of e-mails using second and third-person pronouns consisted of lies.

When people use "you" too much, it is a strategy to give a sense of urgency. This will pique your interest, making you feel as if you are missing out. But as you read through the text or e-mail, you do not see them talking much about themselves and what they can do for you. Chances are, they also lack a concise but thorough introduction about their company. This gives you the idea that they do not have enough details to support their offer.

Also, when people use too many third-person pronouns, this could be a strategy to absolve themselves from the responsibility. It is a trick to get you to blame others just in case the transaction goes wrong.

2. Use of present tense

It has been proven that when liars fabricate information, they rehearse their stories in the present tense. It helps them believe in the characters they create, and it allows their minds to believe in the lies they are about to say. After which, liars will translate their stories into past tense to make them look plausible to listeners and readers. It can even evoke emotion, especially to people who do not know how to determine deception.

But as you read their message, you can see inconsistencies in their writing. It's possible that there is an unnecessary combination of past and present tenses, which gives you the impression that it's all made up. This is proven and tested by psychologists when they found that deceptive people combine present tense with past tense. This is because their brains are making up information, it has no clear definition of whether an event happened in the past or the present. From here, you can see inconsistencies with how people tell stories personally or online.

Observe when people tell the truth, there is consistency in their verb tenses. You may observe them using present tense, but only when they describe how they feel about their experiences. This usually happens to people who were traumatized because they keep reliving the events as they tell the story.

3. The use of concrete information

When people tell the truth, the mind does not put much effort into remembering the details because it already happened. You can observe truthful people share their stories smoothly without delving in too much about the details. This means that they are more abstract in describing their experience.

But when a person is being untruthful, you can observe them disclosing every detail about the situation. This could make reading their stories more difficult because the details are cramped in their sentences or paragraphs. They even include information you don't need to know. It seems to them that the more information they disclose, the easier for you to believe them. But it's quite the opposite. You can see it in their writing when stories and information are not incorporated smoothly. It could mean that they are making things up.

In contrast, you also need to watch out when people disclose too little information. It could mean that they are not prepared for an interrogation or they know that if they tell you more, they can give themselves away.

4. They overemphasize trustworthiness

Ironically, when people add words or phrases that supposedly will make you trust them more, you shouldn't. It's a classic strategy used by liars to make them look convincing. Some of the most common phrases they say are as follows:

- To be honest
- To tell you the truth
- Believe me
- Let's be clear
- The fact is
- Truthfully

Chronic liars use these when they know that they are not as believable. They hope that by overemphasizing their truthfulness, they can convince you of their honesty. It works often, especially for people who do not know these signs.

5. Generalizing

Another common technique that chronic liars use to make people believe them is using general statements such as those starting with "I always" and "I never." These people want to cover their tracks as efficiently as possible. So, they want you to believe that they could never do anything they are accused of. These statements are too good to be true, considering that as humans, no one is perfect. Mistakes, mishaps, and accidents can happen so it's impossible to have a perfect track record.

If someone is being truthful, that person will own up to their mistakes. And they will not generalize their actions. Take a look at the statements below:

A. I've never cheated in my life.
B. I didn't cheat on this one.

Without experience and knowledge, you might think that person A is telling the truth. But no matter how good a person is, there is no such thing as a perfect track record. In this case, person B might just be telling the truth.

6. Deflecting and evading

The next technique you need to know is evading important questions. When interacting personally or online, asking questions is inevitable. And when a person is being truthful, he or she has no problem disclosing what you need to know, especially if it's a matter of urgency. Chronic liars, on the other hand, will avoid difficult questions. Some of the replies you might get include:

- Why do you want to know that?
- That's not important
- What are you talking about?
- Are you accusing me of something?

If people are hesitant to answer your questions, it could be a sign that they're not being truthful.

7. Getting defensive and attacking

Getting defensive is a normal reaction especially when you get blamed for something you didn't do. But it's a different story when you get defensive and attack the people questioning you. Many chronic liars resort to anger and frustration when they get confronted about their actions. They get overly emotional and they tend to make the interrogator look bad. Some of the common sentences or phrases they use are:

- Why don't you believe me?
- How can you doubt me?
- You're wasting my time
- You of all people should understand

Other times, these people will even mention names just to deflect the blame. But when asked why they did it, they make up stories that do not add up.

While these are the most common strategies liars use to get what they want, you should not rely on these red flags alone. Remember, these people are cunning and most of them are highly intelligent. They can upgrade and build new techniques just to get people to believe them.

So, even if they do not meet any of the criteria, it's still best to verify their message by knowing more about the company, the people, and the message. Thankfully, search engines are powerful tools. One-click, and you can find pertinent details about people. But if you do not see matching sources and information, it could be another sign that the person who sent you the text or e-mail is a scammer.

It also does not hurt to crossmatch the information found in their emails with legal files, interviews and direct quotes, including press releases. This will help you verify helpful pieces of information. Look at the timestamps! The news they are telling you today may not even be updated, which is a major giveaway.

Now you know! Not everything you hear from people is the truth. Even when they seem emotional about the situation, it does not mean that they are being truthful. You still need to watch how they speak through their paralanguage and body language to avoid deception. Always find the nose! Remember Pinocchio? Whenever he lies, his nose grows. Every person has a "nose." This is the body part that acts differently when people lie. It could be their hands, eyes, or feet. That's why you need to find your baseline!

You also need to take into account the accuracy of the things you hear or read on the web. Even if people seem legit, you still need to cross-check information and e-mails for any sign of deception. You would not want to be the next victim of a scam.

Do you want more strategies to read people and assess when they are being truthful or not? Read on to the next chapter on speed-reading people and its importance. What do you think is speed-reading and how do you apply it in various situations?

Chapter 7 – Speed-Reading People

How to Read People

There are instances when we are caught off guard by people who mean us harm. We might not be in the mood, or we may feel depressed, or we're just too busy that we neglect to assess people's intentions. Because of this, there is a higher chance we believe what other people are saying, and so, we are easily deceived. This is one of the reasons why we need to learn how to speed-read people.

Speed-reading is a new revolutionary system for communicating. It allows people to instantly grasp other's intentions so one can tailor their approach towards them. Seeing how cunning liars these days are, they use other people's weaknesses to get people's attention and deceive them. They could use one's feelings of sadness, anger, love, and stress just to get people to believe them. Other times, liars also use urgency to deceive people. They could take advantage of one's workload or schedule to get what they want. In these situations, you're more focused on what you're feeling or doing at the moment without paying attention to others' intentions. Chances are, you might only focus on their tone or the movement of their eyes. You neglect to check some of the major giveaways, such as their hands, feet, paralanguage, and many more.

In this chapter, we will discuss how to improve your speed-reading ability further. This way, you can assess when someone is being truthful or not in a shorter period. With the ability to speed-read people, you can tailor your reactions faster, and you will no longer waste your time hearing reasons and propositions from deceivers.

Developing Your Speed-Reading

Almost everyone, at some point in our lives, has tried speed-reading people. Remember when you were a kid, and you were trying to assess if your mom or dad was in a good mood so you can ask for something? Or when you're looking at your teacher's face to see if he or she is likely to give a quiz or not? These are examples of speed-reading people. It is the process of assessing one's temperament, mood, or intentions by looking at their body language, paralanguage, and tone.

When you're trying to assess your parents, teachers, or bosses, you already have a baseline on what they look like when they feel happy or stressed based on experience. But it's a different story when you're dealing with strangers. You have no baseline for their body language and their tone. You may end up victimized by deceivers. Thankfully, experts created the Five C's of Body Language.

This concept consists of cautionary areas that you should consider before ascribing meaning to body language. Apart from the customary meanings of individual body language, you need to consider contexts, clusters, congruence, consistency, and culture. These will help you achieve more accurate information about other's feelings and intentions regardless of the body language they are showing. Let's look into these factors one by one.

1. **Context**

   The first C, context, refers to the external environment. When a stranger walks to you, consider what is going on around you. Where are you located? What happened before that? Where was the person located? What were they doing? Who were they with? What can you infer from their interaction with other people? And what are the reactions of people around you? All of these will give you insight into one's intentions before their approach.

   For example, if a person scratched their nose in a restaurant, it could mean that their nose is itchy. But if they do the same thing in court upon being asked a question, it could indicate that they're lying.

Another example is when a person keeps looking at their watch or the door. When they approach you, you already have an idea about what they might say. They are probably going to borrow your phone to call who he's waiting for. But if the same person does the same body language in a meeting, you can infer that they might be anxious or that they are eager to leave the room.

2. **Clusters**

The next C is cluster. This refers to the combination of body language. Instead of focusing on one act and ascribing a heavy meaning to it, consider looking for clusters to give you a more accurate read. Experts recommend looking for more than three body language signs when speed-reading people.

For example, when you see someone sweating, blinking rapidly, shifting weight from one foot to the other, fidgeting, or breathing heavily, you can infer that a person is anxious. But if you put a heavy meaning to only one or two body language, such as sweating or breathing heavily, you might infer that a person may only be tired.

3. Congruence
The next factor you need to consider is congruence. This refers to the correspondence of one's body movements. It means that what they say corresponds to their non-verbal cues. For example, if they say they are happy, their eyes, hands, and posture should show the same. If not, it could indicate that they're lying.

For this aspect, you need to review the meanings of each body language. This will give you a better understanding of others' feelings and intentions.

When you see one's body language and posture, you already have an idea about what others are feeling. However, if it is matched by a contradicting non-verbal cue coming from their arms, legs, plus facial expressions, it could indicate a different meaning. Let's take a look at some of the incongruent body language that people make that can give their feelings and thoughts away.

We already discussed the meaning of arm-crossing and leg-crossing. Now, if you match this with a closed spine position, it could indicate boredom, disinterest, and disconnection. This also connotes hostility which could discourage discussion. But if you match arm-crossing and leg-crossing with an open posture, it could assert dominance and authority. It could also mean concentration and thinking.

Putting your hands in your pockets is also a sign of a closed posture. It could mean that you are doubtful and that you lack confidence. Matched with an open posture, it could mean arrogance or over-confidence, which could either make or break your first impression with other people.

We also discussed how putting your hands at the front or at the back has different meanings. If you match it with a closed spine, it could mean submissiveness, guilt, respect, or anxicty. But if you match it with an open spine position, it can indicate authority and dominance.

They also discuss the meaning of fidgeting hands and legs. Its negative meaning could be exaggerated when you match it with a closed posture. It could mean that you're eager for the conversation to be over and that you have somewhere else to be.

Now let's pair up facial expressions with posture.

In the last chapter, we discussed eye gaze in which a person looks directly into your eyes while having a conversation. Normally, this would indicate that they're interested and are paying attention. However, when it is matched with a closed spine position, and the person is leaning towards you, it could be threatening and distracting. This is commonly used by con artists when they want to distract you from your thoughts. Instead of letting you think properly, they use this body language to distract you and hinder you from making a good decision. Conversely, if eye gazing is matched with an open spine position, it could mean that a person is undermining you or is feeling superior over you.

We also discussed blinking, which is a natural reflex of people. However, increased blinking could indicate anxiety or lying. But if it is matched by a closed spine position, it could mean that a person is tired or is guilty of something. But when he or she starts to lean towards you and blink at your profusely, it could mean mockery or ridicule.

The next is lip-biting which is usually a symbol of interest or flirting. But if it is matched with a closed posture, it could indicate doubt, guilt, or lack of self-confidence. If it is matched with an open posture, it could mean excitement or anticipation.

Another gesture is covering the mouth. Usually, this means that a person is in shock or is respectfully covering their cough or yawn. But if it is matched with a closed posture, it could indicate that a person may be in pain physically or emotionally. Conversely, if the person does this with an open position, it could indicate relief or joy.

We also discussed the meaning when a person places their hands on their hips. When this is matched with a closed position and the person is leaning towards you, it could be an attempt to hear you better when you're explaining or that person is trying to intimidate you more. However, if it is matched with an open posture, it could indicate that a person is showing that they are dominant and superior over you.

There are many other combinations you need to watch out for. This is why it is important to review the meanings of body language and other non-verbal cues.

4. Consistency

The fourth C you need to know when reading people's body language is consistency. It is important to look for patterns of behavior to create a baseline. For example, when you observe someone holding their head in their hands, you might think they're bored or sleepy. This usually happens in the classroom, and many teachers see this as a sign of disrespect. But as you get to know the student, you can see that this is just a way for them to concentrate on the discussion.

The same is true when you observe people who cross their arms often. At first, you may think that they have a closed mindset or that they are asserting dominance. But as you interact with them, you see that it is their habit.

5. Culture

The last but not the least factor to consider when speed-reading people is culture. We reiterated in the previous chapters that culture plays an important role in how one acts, speaks, and thinks.

So, before you ascribe any meaning to someone's body language, understand their culture.

Techniques to Speed-Read People

Now that we have established the five factors that could affect the meaning of body language, we can now delve into five of the most effective techniques to speed-read people. Luckily, an FBI agent, LaRae Quy, was willing to share his secrets in speed-reading people after 23 years in service. According to him, learning how to read others will greatly affect how you deal with them. You can adapt your communication style to make sure your message is received in the best way possible.

Some of you might be thinking, "I don't have what it takes to become an interrogator, much less to figure out what someone is thinking in an instant." But according to our FBI agent, people do not need to be top-notch interrogators to figure out what's on others' minds. There will always be signs but you need to know what you're looking for. So here are his techniques for speed-reading people:

1. Creating a baseline
   The technique that they have been discussing since the beginning of the book is actually proven and tested by FBI agents. This is why before you read

people, you need to have a clear picture of how they act when they're relaxed. This way, you can pinpoint changes in their behavior when the context changes.

2. Mirroring
   Everyone has mirror neurons. These are built-in monitors inside our brains that reflect what others are thinking or feeling. This is why when we see someone we like, we smile at each other to show our fondness. Conversely, when you see someone you hate, you will frown, and the person in front of you is likely to mimic your reaction.

   When you're trying to assess when someone is being truthful or not, use your mirror neurons. Try to smile at them. If they reciprocate your facial expression, it could mean that they're sincere and genuine. But if they don't reciprocate, it could mean that there is a disconnect or disinterest between you.

3. Identify the strong voice
   Despite what people think, the most powerful person in the room is not always seated at the head of the table. They are the most confident people. Observe when you're in a conference room. The most confident and outspoken

one catches your attention above all else, including the leader or the head of the company.

This could mean that the leader has a weaker personality and may not even be open to your suggestions. If you're trying to pitch in ideas, the best person to share this with is the most confident for the most powerful person in the room. While this person may not have the position of power, he or she has the people power which comes from the support of their colleagues. In most cases, this supersedes position power.

4. Observing how they walk
   This may come as a shock but observing how people walk makes a difference in assessing what's on their mind. Consider their posture. Is their spine in a C-shaped position? If so, they might not be confident, or they might have a weaker personality. You can also observe that they lack a flowing motion. Meaning, their body language is limited and hidden so their movements look stiff and jerky. But if they embody an open posture, it means that they are confident, powerful, and have a strong personality.

If you're in a meeting or conference, watch out for people who embody a confident posture. It could mean that they have lots of ideas in mind, but they're just waiting for the right moment to speak up. If you're the head of the meeting, consider asking them direct questions to pique their mind and pull great ideas out into the open.

5. Pinpointing action words
   According to FBI agents, words are the best way to get into someone's head. Words represent thoughts, so it would help to pinpoint action words or verbs to get clues about one's personality.

   For example, your boss said, "We decided to merge."

   From this statement, the action word is "decided." This single word could indicate that your boss is not impulsive, thinks things through, and weighs their choices. And the fact that they used "we" could mean that they are team-oriented.

   Compare it to this statement: "We want to merge." From this statement, you can infer assertiveness and arrogance.

   It may seem that these action words are just part of the sentence. Little do you know the difference it makes when interacting with other people.

6. Look for personality clues
    Each of us have different personalities. You may think that these do not show at first glance. But in reality, a person is overflowing with clues that give away parts of their personality.

    Posture alone will give you an insight into whether a person is introverted or extroverted. You can also derive someone's personality based on their makeup, clothing, hairdo, phone case, bag, and many more. Although these are superficial signs, they can give you clues about the person you are dealing with.

7. Listen intently
    The last but not the least technique you can use to speed-read people is listening intently. Consider what they say and how they say it. How fast and loud do they talk? Sometimes, when a person speaks loudly, it could mean that they want to catch your attention, to feel more important, or to emphasize or prove something. It could also be that they are anxious and shy. But often, it's how they are raised, or it's in their biology to have a loud voice.

    But what about if a person talks too fast? It could mean that they are thinking too fast that they are trying to keep up with their thoughts. They feel that if they don't talk quickly, they might lose their train of thought. Another reason why people speak fast is nervousness and anxiety. Some people want the conversation to be over with. But sadly, it is at the expense of clarity and understanding.

These are only some of the proven and tested ways to speed-read people in various situations. But what about if a person is wearing a mask and wearing a thick coat or jacket. In this case, it's difficult to assess what's on other people's minds because you cannot see their facial expressions or their body gestures.

There is a trending meme where people claim to have mastered the fake smile underneath their masks. They can squint their eyes to show smiling and welcoming eyes but inside the mask, there is a frown. So, how do you determine when a person is being truthful or when they are being friendly or not? Here are some tips to speed-read people behind a mask.

1. Watch out for squinted eyes
   When you see people squinting to show that they are smiling, watch the creases around their eyes. If a person is truly smiling, you can see wrinkles

around the eyes. But if a person is merely squinting, you can see a smoother appearance around the eyes. This could mean that a person doesn't like you or doesn't like what's going on. It could also mean that they disagree with what you're saying.

2. Another sign is touching the neck. This is a macro-activity that gives people away even if they're wearing masks or thick clothes. It could mean that they are struggling with something or that they are stressed and concerned about the situation.

   If you see someone touching their neck dimple or the visible indentation at the front of the neck, it could mean that a person is distressed or insecure. If you notice this, try communicating with them with more empathy to help ease their anxiety.

3. Rubbing the chest. This is another sign that a person is stressed or anxious. If a person is rubbing the upper part of their chest with a palm or their fingers, it could indicate concern or discomfort. It could also mean a lack of confidence.

4. Watch the brows
   Since you can't see their lips, one way to assess when a person is welcoming or not is through their eyebrows. When someone arches their eyebrows, it means that they are happy to see you or that they are pleasantly surprised.

   But if you see them raising one eyebrow, it could mean disinterest, discomfort, disbelief, or disapproval.

5. Tilted head
   The last but not the least body language to check when someone's wearing a mask is head positioning. If people tilt their heads, it could mean that they are interested in what's going on and that they are fully present. It could also mean that they agree with what you're saying.

   There are so many ways to speed-read people. The signs are already there. But you have to let your subconscious play its part. As we have discussed in the previous chapters, it is important to trust your gut. Even when there is no visible proof, chances are, your gut is correct.

So, even if you're not going to act on it, listen to what your instinct has to say. Because this means that your subconscious already did prior research about the person you are reading.

It is also important to sense emotional energy. This refers to the vied that people give off. Although there is no solid proof or outcome of this vibe, you can feel your body tingling with it. Feel your goosebumps, and don't shy them away. If you feel like your energy is being drained by a person, it signals you to break the connection.

Lastly, consider flashes of insight or "aha" moments. Stay alert of any sign and red flag. Don't discount them just because someone apologizes or makes it up to you. This includes their handshake, hug, or touch. They may claim it's accidental, but it might actually be giving you the information you need about that person. Speed-reading is so interesting, don't you think? You can use all of your senses, including your emotional radar. This leaves us to think, "Can you use your emotional intelligence to speed-read people? Read on to the next chapter about emotional intelligence, its importance, and how you can improve it.

Chapter 8 – Are You Emotionally Intelligent?

What Does it Mean to be Emotionally Intelligent?

When reading people's behavior and intentions, you are not only focusing on the physical movements they show. You also focus on the emotions they exude. This is the reason why you get "vibes" from other people. It is a manifestation of their feelings at that moment. Mostly, you can detect when a vibe is negative or positive. But you can never fully interpret what they mean unless you have emotional intelligence.

Emotional intelligence refers to the ability to recognize the emotions of oneself and other people. EQ also refers to one's ability to understand, use, and manage their emotions to relieve stress, communicate effectively, empathize with others, and overcome challenges. It is an important aspect of mankind that helps achieve goals career-wise, relationship-wise, and other personal aspects.

Besides, emotional intelligence also helps you connect with your emotions, put your intentions into action, and make educated choices about what matters to you. According to experts, emotional intelligence has four attributes:

1. Self-Management

If one is emotionally intelligent, they can display self-management skills which is the ability to control impulsive feelings and behavior in any given situation. Self-control is a vital part of this because it makes people control their impulses and temperament even when they are faced with difficulties.

2. Self-Awareness

Next is self-awareness, which is the process of acknowledging your weaknesses and strengths along with the strategies you can employ for improvement. With self-awareness, you also understand who you are, taking into account your personality, values, and principles. It helps you clarify your thoughts and intentions, allowing you to make sound decisions in taking a course of action.

3. Social Awareness

Another attribute of emotional intelligence is social awareness. This entails showing empathy to other people. With social awareness, a person can understand other people's emotions, needs, concerns, and intentions. If you have this skill, it makes it easier for you to pick up emotional cues or "vibes" and interpret them accurately, which is one of the most important aspects of speed-reading.

4. **Relationship Management**
   The last but not the least attribute of emotional intelligence is relationship management. This is the ability to form mutually beneficial relationships with others. With this skill, you understand how to build and sustain positive relationships, connect effectively, empower and influence others, collaborate effectively, and resolve conflict.

Emotional intelligence should not be mistaken for positive traits such as calmness and motivation. These characteristics are only some of the traits that an emotionally intelligent person will exude. According to studies, emotional intelligence is a skill. It's an ability acquired over time due to one's age and experience. It allows people to be wiser in dealing with their emotions as they mature.

Many people discount emotional intelligence as an important aspect of achieving success. Most are too preoccupied with improving their intelligence quotient or IQ, and they neglect to enhance their ability to manage their emotions. But in real life, it doesn't matter how intelligent you are. What matters, in the end, is how you deal with people.

This is evident in the hiring and selection process in many organizations. Most companies hire people with high emotional quotients rather than those with high intelligent quotients. According to them, you can teach skill, but you cannot impart personality, which, to them, is very important in teamwork. This is but one of the advantages of having a high emotional IQ.

Aside from that, this ability can also help people excel in school and work. With emotional intelligence, you can easily deal with narcissistic and arrogant people and prevent them from getting under your skin.

With high EQ, a person can easily get along with others, giving them more opportunities to learn from the experiences of other people.

Another benefit of having a high EQ is physical health. Believe it or not, this skill can affect several diseases such as heart ailments, diabetes, and many more. The body and mind are a system. What affects one will reflect on the other. When someone is anxious, they can experience physiological manifestations such as butterflies in the stomach, sweating, and shaking. Conversely, when one is depressed, they also experience heartache. This is proven by doctors when they found that people with depression have uncommonly sticky platelets. This accelerates atherosclerosis or the hardening of arteries, which increases the chance of heart attack.

The inability to cope with stress is also correlated to diabetes. It's no surprise that people resort to binge eating whenever they're upset, stressed, or apprehended. Without exercise, this can lead to obesity, and over time, diabetes.

People with high emotional intelligence also have a lower risk of psychological disorders such as depression and anxiety. According to experts, prolonged stress and the inability to cope with it can lead to mental health issues. Without intervention, it could lead to severe disorders that cause dysfunctionality in someone's life.

Raising Your Emotional Intelligence

Seeing how important emotional intelligence is, it is your obligation to yourself to raise your EQ. Not only will this help you manage your emotions, but it will also allow you to break free from all your emotional and psychological limits that keep you from achieving your goals.

Luckily, psychologist Marc Brackett, the founder of Yale Center for Emotional Intelligence found that there are ways to increase one's emotional intelligence. He developed a system around the acronym RULER, which has been used in over 2000 schools worldwide to teach about emotional intelligence. Without further ado, here are five skills you need to practice now to improve your EQ:

Recognize

The first step to control your emotions is to recognize them. Many people make the mistake of ignoring their feelings and burying them deeply. Little do they know that this is merely a temporary solution to keep your emotions at bay. Over time, the emotions you bury will haunt you, and it will have a greater impact on your mental health.

It is important to recognize your emotions so you can face them head-on. If you're sad, angry, or frustrated, don't shy away from the situation. Instead, let them out. Acknowledge that they exist even if you don't know the reason for it. This will help you understand what the problem is so you can solve it from the roots.

If you're confused about your emotions, you can use the mood meter as recommended by Brackett. The Mood Meter can help you assess what you're feeling in the moment to give you insight into your problem.

Understand

The next step to achieve emotional intelligence is to understand your emotions. Ask yourself why you're feeling that way. What happened prior to your feelings? Who was involved in the situation? What memories do you remember that may have aggravated your feelings?

Understanding these causes will give you clues on how to address them. For example, someone said that you're irresponsible. Normally, you would not get offended by it because you don't usually care about what other people think. But all of a sudden, you feel so affected by it now. The first step is to recognize that you're feeling frustrated. Now, understand why. Who said it to you? When was the last time you were told you're irresponsible? Did anything happen today that set you off in a bad mood? Consider all of these factors to determine the root of your feelings so you can tackle them.

Label

It's not enough to identify and understand an emotion; we can also benefit from finding the appropriate words to express it. There are thousands of words in the English dictionary. Use them to label what you're feeling. It's not enough to say you're feeling stressed or frustrated. It's best to be as specific as possible. Instead of saying, "I feel frustrated," you can say, "I'm angry at the person who said I'm irresponsible."

Saying "frustrated" alone could mean other things. If you don't specify it, it could derail you from assessing the real problem and creating a solution for it.

Express

After putting a label on your feelings, it is important to express them. Although there are times when you cannot convey them right away, never neglect to express your emotions in your own way. You can talk to a friend, a colleague, or a family member. You can write it in your journal or paint it out. You can even watch drama to help you bring your emotions out. But if you plan to convey your emotions directly to the person who has wronged you, make sure you do it proactively and respectfully so you don't say or do things you might regret.

Regulate

The final emotional ability is figuring out how to deal with our emotions. Regulating our emotions entails coping with them in a way that helps you calm down and work your feelings out. This does not imply suppressing our emotions. Rather, regulation entails learning to embrace and manage them effectively. There are many ways to regulate emotion. You can sleep or take a nap. You can listen to music or play games. Your goal now is to go back to your normal emotional state and move on with your life.

Many make the mistake of jumping from R to R. Meaning upon recognizing, they immediately move forward to regulation. While this seems to be the healthiest route, it could have a tremendous impact on your emotional well-being. This means that you were unable to express your emotions properly. It also means that you were unable to identify the problem and create a solution for it. If this happens, your emotions will haunt you one day and may cause more challenging circumstances.

Now that you have learned how you can increase your emotional intelligence, let's see what describes people with high EQ. This will help you monitor your behavior and identify points for improvement.

9 Signs That You Have High Emotional Intelligence

Sign 1: Accountable

People with low emotional intelligence are often prone to making excuses. They blame others and their environment for their mistakes. These people do not take accountability for their actions which can only lead to unproductivity and demotivation.

Conversely, people with high EQ are eager to hear feedback—positive or negative. They take this constructively and use it to improve themselves.

Sign 2: Open-minded

Emotionally intelligent people are always open to suggestions. They do not shut people off. Chances are that these people will still listen out of respect to the speaker. Also, they are willing to change their minds and assimilate information, especially when they hear better ideas from other people.

Sign 3: Active listeners

The third characteristic that describes people with high emotional intelligence is being active listeners. When these people listen, they do it intently. They focus on understanding what is being said and the emotion that comes with it. As active listeners, emotionally intelligent people also know how to separate their biases and prevent them from clouding their judgment. This is why emotionally intelligent people make outstanding therapists, counselors, leaders, teachers, and businessmen. They take into account all verbal and non-verbal cues of their clients to give the best service to them.

Sign 4: Demonstrate Empathy

Empathy, or the ability to acknowledge and comprehend others' thoughts and emotions, allows you to communicate with others on a deeper level. Rather than passing judgment or assigning labels to others, you strive to see things from their perspective. Empathy does not always imply agreement with another person's viewpoint. Instead, it's about attempting to comprehend, which helps you form deeper, and more fulfilling bonds.

Sign 5: They don't sugarcoat the truth

Emotionally intelligent people can tell people the truth while considering other people's feelings. They know how to read non-verbal cues which could indicate if a person is in a bad or good mood. They also pick up on hints easily which allows them to determine the right time to tell people good or bad news. This way, they don't aggravate people's feelings which could lead to impulsive behavior.

Sign 6: They apologize

To be willing to say "I'm sorry" requires bravery and courage. It also displays modesty which is evident among emotionally intelligent people.

When they know they're wrong, people with high emotional intelligence don't waste time trying to prove they're right. Rather than making excuses, they deliver a straightforward and sincere apology to the people they wronged. And after the situation, they will learn from the experience and change for the better.

Sign 7: Forgive and forget

Holding a grudge is another effect of holding your feelings in and not expressing them. It's like carrying a ton of cement on your chest. It's heavy and difficult to bear. Often, non-forgiveness makes people do inappropriate things that could aggravate their problems.

People with high emotional intelligence know better. Instead of grudges, they learn to forgive and move on even without an apology. It's not that the person who wronged them is off the hook. The reason why they choose to forgive is to set themselves free from the burden of anger and frustration. This allows them to heal and move forward with their lives.

Sign 8: Desire to help others succeed and succeed for themselves

Some people try to bring everyone down so they can rise to the top. Emotionally intelligent people are different. They're the complete opposite of condescending people. Instead of pulling people down, their security allows them to push people up to help them achieve their goals. Emotionally intelligent people will even act as a beacon to motivate others to achieve their goals. They do not think about the rewards of their actions because to them, the best reward is the joy of helping and seeing others succeed.

Sign 9: Showing authenticity

In this day and age, many people need to belong even if it means sacrificing their principles and giving up the people who truly believe them. Emotionally intelligent people are different. They are secure about themselves, their values, and principles. These people are strong enough to stand alone, especially if it means upholding their principles and values. Belonging to a group does not mean much to them, especially if it means changing their personality and discarding what they believe. Knowing how secure they are, they already form a support system consisting of people as emotionally intelligent as them.

Can you imagine becoming emotionally intelligent? This means you no longer have to put up with other people's negativities because you are mature enough to ignore them. With emotional intelligence, there is peace and tranquility. Rather than focusing on hate, anxiety, and anger, you will learn to let these feelings go and just focus on your goals. If you come to think of it, building emotional intelligence is one of the most vital ways to break free from the chains of society and finally transcend.

Apart from these benefits, emotional intelligence also helps you avoid being victimized by manipulators, liars, and condescending people. How? Read on to the next chapter.

Chapter 9 – Protecting Yourself Against Dark Influence and Manipulation

While emotional intelligence helps ward off manipulation, it does not stop people from trying their best to get what they want from you. No matter how much you try to avoid liars, scams, or deceivers, someone will always come your way to challenge your emotions by breaking them to make you their little puppet. This is why it is important to protect yourself against dark influence and manipulation.

How Does Dark Influence and Manipulation Work?

Dark psychology encompasses dark influence and manipulation. It is the science and art of mind control. This shouldn't be confused with psychology, which is the study of human behavior and is central to a person's thoughts, actions, and interactions. Dark psychology is a phenomenon by which people use motivation, persuasion, manipulation, and coercion to get what they want.

People who use dark influence attack others' mental and emotional states to get what they want. They seek imbalance of power, and they take advantage of people's weaknesses to get control, benefits, and privileges. The worst part about dark influence is it often happens in close relationships. This is because the manipulator already knows what drives the victim. They already know their weaknesses, so it's easy for them to manipulate their thoughts and feelings.

However, manipulation can also happen in casual relationships. It could be in the form of blackmailing, feigning ignorance or innocence, lying, denying, blaming, gaslighting, withholding information, isolating people, implicit threatening, and many more.

This leaves the question, "Are people born to be manipulators, or are they conditioned? This is yet again another question of nurture vs. nature. While we all know that nurture has a large impact on one's behavior, we shouldn't discount genetics. Research has already proven that there are biological anomalies within people with antisocial behaviors. This means that a person could be predisposed to grow up with destructive behaviors. And if this is matched with a hostile environment where a person needs to survive your manipulation, their tendency to display antisocial behaviors will be increased.

Psychologists have come up with the "Dark Triad." This consists of factors that can help authorities and doctors predict if a person has manipulative properties. Here are some of the indicators:

a. Narcissism
Clinically diagnosed narcissistic people have inflated self-worth. They need to be validated for being superior. They want to be worshipped and adored. Whatever they want, they feel they are entitled to it and that people should give it to them no matter the expense. These people have no problem using dark psychology to get what they want. The worst part is these people seem so sweet and charming in the beginning. But as you trust them, you'll see how fast they can drain the life and resources out of you.

b. Machiavellianism
In psychology, this refers to a personality trait in which a person is focused on their needs above all else. This is why they are prepared to manipulate, deceive, and exploit others to get what they want.

c. Psychopathy
This is defined as a mental disorder wherein an individual manifests immoral and antisocial behavior. These people express extreme egocentricity. They don't follow norms and laws, and they

are unable to establish meaningful relationships.

Sociopathy, on the other hand, is commonly interchanged with psychopathy. It is a trait that defines someone who is without conscience. It is a description of people who are hateful or hate-worthy.

To differentiate the two, sociopaths make it clear that they don't care what you feel. They behave angrily and impulsively. And when they do something wrong, they recognize it, but they rationalize their behavior. Sociopaths also cannot maintain regular work and family life. They find it difficult to form deep connections with people.

Psychopaths, on the other hand, pretend to care. However, they display cold-hearted behavior. They cannot recognize other people's distress, and they are likely to build shallow and fake relationships. These people maintain a normal life so they can cover any criminal activity. They can love people in their own way, but they still prioritize what they need and continue committing crimes and other immoral behaviors.

If you think these are the only people who can use dark manipulation, think again. Almost everyone around you can do it, especially those who you might idolize or admire. Examples of this are attorneys whose only goal is to win their case. Often, they resort to dark persuasion and manipulation to get what they want. Politicians also use dark psychology to get people to believe in them and to vote for them. Other examples include salespeople and public speakers who want to use their persuasion skills to get you to buy their products or believe what they are saying. Many people might deny this. But if they look closely at the lengths they are willing to go to get what they want, there's no doubt that at some point, they used dark psychology. This leaves the question what is going through their head when they manipulate? Is it intentional or unintentional? Let's find out.

A Peek into the Head of These Malicious People

There's no doubt that each of us has encountered a manipulative experience. It could be from a family member, a friend, a romantic partner, a colleague, or even a stranger. When we figure out that we were just manipulated or coerced, we feel angry and frustrated. Sometimes we blame ourselves for putting up with their behavior and for letting it go on for so long. This anger could lead to depression and anxiety, which, over time, can cause dysfunction in your life. One way to help you cope with the anger you are feeling is to understand what's happening within the mind of the manipulator. What were they thinking, and how is their brain wired?

Thinking about these questions, the most common answers are:

"because they are bad people..."

"some people are just like that..."

"because they are evil psychopaths..."

But if you fully analyze the situation, don't you think that they are victims too? Are they really evil or are they made to be evil? Earlier, we discussed the dark triad and the people who are more likely to display manipulative acts. This includes people with Narcissism, Machiavellianism, and Antisocial Personality Disorders. Let's look at the main causes of these psychological disorders.

Narcissism

Narcissistic personality disorder is a mental condition in which people have an inflated sense of importance. When you encounter these people, chances are, you judge them, and you avoid them. And with good reason!

Because of their ruthless personality, they can manipulate you or insult you, which can only ruin your day. But have you ever asked yourself the root of narcissism? It could change how you view others with the disorder.

In one school of thought, psychologists believe that narcissism is a result of insecurity as a child. It could be that their parents didn't give them enough attention, so they compensated for this when they grew older. It's also possible that they grew up having nothing. As a child, they could be jealous of other kids for having fancy objects they couldn't have. And so, as adults, they prey on others' resources to get what they want.

In another theory, psychologists believe that narcissism is a product of abuse. Because of this, narcissism has become their defense mechanism to block out what hurts or what terrifies them. Over time, this narcissistic personality got the best of them and they ended up embodying it fully.

Because of these experiences, people with narcissistic personalities find it difficult to grasp the concepts of healthy relationships. To them, having relationships could only hurt them. So, before people can, they do it first. It's also possible that all their lives, having relationships is the only way they get through life. And because of the rewards, they no longer focus on the connections, only the shallow and materialistic aspects of partnership.

Machiavellianism

As discussed, Machiavellianism is a trait that describes people who are so focused on their own interests. Some of the signs that one has a Machiavellian personality are as follows:

- Focused on getting what they want
- Prioritizes money and power over relationships
- Comes across as confident
- They lie and deceive to get what they want
- They come across as aloof and difficult to get to know
- Low levels of empathy
- Lack of warmth in social interactions

When people come across Machiavellians, the first word that comes to mind is heartless because the above statements are what they see. But they don't know that people who have a high Machiavellianism trait are also:

- Lonely
- Possibly depressed
- Anxious
- Confused
- Insecure

Sometimes, people use Machiavellianism as a defense mechanism. Because they have been beaten up by life, they forget all the good things about it, such as love, companionship, and intimacy. These people may have been victims of extreme poverty, to the point where they had to fight tooth and nail for a piece of grain. It's also possible that they are victims of abuse as children. They adapted the Machiavellian mindset to protect themselves from people who can hurt them and prevent themselves from experiencing the hardships they experienced before. It's probably why they prioritize power and money, so they feel secure that they will never go poor again.

It's sad, really. These people make you think that they are strong and capable on the outside. But on the inside, they are as confused and lonely as anybody else. They crave attention and intimacy. But they're afraid that if they let their guards down, it could derail them from their plan. This gives them fear and apprehension. That's why they prefer being alone and disconnected from other people.

Psychopathy

The third and last aspect in the triad is psychopaths. They are the rule breakers of society. Yet, behind that tough exterior is a beaten person. Psychologists have proven that people who develop psychopathy have been exposed to dysfunctional environments as early as childhood. They may have been abused, neglected, or separated from their parents at an early age. This is why they did not have any guidance about the dos and don'ts of life.

Poor bonding with parents is also a common factor of psychopathy. It's possible that their parents have mental health issues of their own, or they have substance abuse problems that cause a disconnect between them and their children. Lastly, it could be that these children have unresolved traumas which continue to haunt them even as adults.

These causes do not justify the fact that what they're doing is wrong. However, it gives you an idea about where they are coming from. It could help alleviate the anger and frustration you're feeling. And instead of resorting to self-blame, you will realize that life can be cruel, and some could not cope as well as they should. No one can avoid these people. So, the best way to deal with manipulators is to develop a discerning eye.

Developing a Discerning Eye

There are several red flags to watch out for that indicate whether a person tends to manipulate you. Here are some of the most common signs that a person belongs to the Dark Triad:

1. *They take pleasure in other people's misfortune.*
   These people like to stir the pot. And when it goes badly for one person, they enjoy it. They like to see the drama and the commotion of people fighting. Sometimes, you can even see them enjoying hearing terrible news.

2. *They make you uncomfortable*
   Although there is no solid proof that they are a part of the dark triad, they give off this creepy and uncomfortable vibe. Listen to your gut. It's probably telling you to run as far away as you can.

3. *Being mean to animals*
   Psychologists have proven that mean and cruel people to animals are likely to belong to the dark triad.

4. *Using humor as an insult*
   When you get offended by it, they eventually say, "Relax, it's just a joke."

5. *They lie all the time*
   They scam people to get what they want. Plus, they use deception to hide who they truly are.

6. *They belittle your fears*
   They joke about your fears despite your strong feelings toward it. Instead of

giving comfort, they will give you ridicule, and they make you feel stupid for feeling terrified.

7. *They don't feel guilt*
Even if they know they are at fault, they do not care. You won't hear an apology from them.

8. *Lacks empathy*
They don't feel for others' emotions. They don't care if you're sad or grieving. All you wanted to do was give them what they want.

9. *Being racist or sexist*
They believe that some people are more superior to others. And when others are victims of racism or sexism, they would blame the minorities and ridicule them.

10. *They need to be in control*
These people like to be in control of things. If not, they tend to react harshly and impulsively.

11. *They have a reputation*
You may already be hearing negative stories about them. Even when you don't want to judge, consider the truthfulness behind the story and watch your back.

12. *They believe that everything is about them*
Even when an event does not concern them, they make it a habit to butt in and try to turn the whole scene towards them.

13. *They're inconsistent*
You can observe them changing their statements, perspectives, and attitudes in an instant, especially when it helps them get what they want.

14. *They want you to prove yourself to them*
Another red flag that you need to watch out for is they want you to prove your loyalty to them. You can observe that some of the requests are too difficult and unreasonable. This may include choosing between your family or them. Despite doing the things they want, they continuously seek negativity. Hence, they have a reason to ask for more assurance from you.

15. *They make you defend yourself*
The last but not the least red flag is making you defend yourself. Even when they're not interested in your point of view, they want you to continue defending yourself. These people will listen to every word you say to look for mistakes and question you for them.

5 Ways to Protect Yourself

Seeing how exhausting it is to deal with manipulators and toxic people, it is important to learn how to protect yourself from them. Here are some of the ways:

1. **Avoid giving them the attention they want**
   This is a common solution, when you're dealing with narcissists. If you don't give them the attention they want, chances are, they will leave you alone. As much as possible, do not instigate and do not confront them no matter how irritating they are. These people don't know that they have a problem. Their brains are hardwired to think grandiosity. If you confront them, you will not get a healthy response. They will turn the situation around to make you look stupid or to make you feel awful.

2. **Cut your ties**
   If you observe that the person you're dealing with belongs to the dark triad, cut your ties immediately, or at the very least, keep your distance. Do not pretend that what they're doing is OK. There's nothing OK with manipulation and deception. If you're starting to feel toxicity or you suspect it, it's best to keep your distance. You can make up some

reason why you need to go to work or home. You could also go with other people so they don't try to victimize you.

3. **Never let your guard down**
   These people can "smell" your fear and your weakness. So, if you suspect manipulation, never let your guard down. Do not tell them important details about your life. Once they fish for enough information, they will use it to manipulate you.

4. **Don't let them lie.**
   One of the techniques that people use when dealing with manipulators is to play along with the deception. They make it fun. However, not everyone can banter playfully with manipulators, especially if they have anxiety or if they are under a lot of stress.

   When you play along with a manipulator, make sure you don't get attached. These people can get so charming. Even when you think you're playing them, it might be the other way around.

5. **Ignore insults and negativity**
   Some manipulators use insult to get your attention, especially if it means creating drama. During these situations, remember that it's not the people talking,

it's the demons inside them. Try to stay calm as much as possible because if you show anger or frustration, they will fuel it up and cause you more trouble.

6. **Beware of false kindness**
Some people get deceived because they believe in the slightest change of perspective or attitude from these people. You can't blame them. Some people are hay wired to look at the positive side and hope that a person can change. It's not the same story to people who belong to the dark triad. These people do not even know that they have personality disorders. They don't care about their reputation. It's safe to say that they are callous. Spending a day with them will not change who they are. They need psychological treatment, in fact, a series of them, to help them change their perceptions in life. So, if they show you some kindness such as honesty or protection, don't believe them. This could be their modus to get you to trust them.

Manipulation does not only come from strangers. The most painful form of manipulation comes from your friends and loved ones. It might be difficult to be with them, but it's also difficult to keep your distance. But you need to remember to respect yourself enough to walk away. Dealing with manipulators can take a toll on your mental health. So, before they cause permanent damage, you need to choose yourself first and move on. Remember what Karl Marx said, there comes a time when you need to let go of pointless drama, and the people who create it. The best way to have a fulfilling life is to surround yourself with the people who truly love you and gives you the support and care you need.

Chapter 10 – More on People with Dark Personality

Manipulators and liars are not the only people with dark personalities. There are more people you need to worry about who are far worse than these people—criminals. These people include rapists, arsonists, thieves, and murderers, among others. They can do far worse than manipulators and liars. This is why it is essential to tell them apart from others. Criminal behavior is one of the most difficult topics to discuss because various factors affect the situation. But generally, a criminal act occurs when there is a motive, a means, and an opportunity.

Know Who You are Facing Against

According to research, there are specific criminal behaviors that lead offenders to push through with a crime. These are called risk factors or criminogenic needs. One way to understand criminal behavior is to understand criminogenic needs. These needs are traits associated with criminal thinking. It is also dynamically defined as the crime-producing factors that increase the risk of criminality.

But before we delve into criminogenic needs, it is important to understand the deeper root of criminality. Apart from environmental or external factors, psychologists believe that criminality can start with biology and genetics.

Biological risk factors are defined as anything that "impinges on the child from conception to birth." Parents who possess criminogenic needs can pass these traits to their children. According to psychologists, these genetic predispositions also play a role in shaping the environment. Genes influence how parents raise their children. In turn, genes affect the responses that children evoke to their external environment. It has also been found that genetics can define an individual's ability to control temperament, confidence, empathy, and impulsivity.

Let's move forward to criminogenic needs. As discussed, these are traits that a person possesses that lead to criminal behavior. And according to psychology, there are six criminogenic needs:

1. Antisocial values
    This refers to one's criminal thinking. It includes criminal rationalization, which makes people believe that their criminal behavior is justified. People who possess this trait usually blame others for negative behavior. They see nothing wrong with how they think or act. Hence, they show no remorse.

2. Criminal peers
   Another factor that can lead to criminal behavior is having criminal peers. This is not a surprise due to the influence of other people. If they see others who think and act like them, they feel like they belong. These criminal peers act like their support system, and it makes it okay for them to commit criminal acts.

3. Antisocial personality
   These traits involve atypical behavior prior to the age of 15. Some of these behaviors include running away, getting into fights, skipping school, possessing weapons, lying, stealing, and causing property damage.

4. Dysfunctional family
   Psychologists have proven that criminality's most common risk factor is lack of family support, financially or emotionally. If a person's family cannot solve problems and communicate effectively, this could affect how one thinks. It could make someone callous to survive.

5. Low self-control
   This refers to one's inability to control their impairment or impulsivity. These people do not plan or think before acting.

Their mindset lies on "now" rather than the consequences later.

6. Substance abuse
The last but not the least criminogenic need is substance abuse. This includes the use of drugs and alcohol that significantly affects how one engages in a productive lifestyle. Because of continuous usage, they could develop tolerance to the substance which will make them need more to become intoxicated. This abuse drives people to commit further acts of criminal activity.

Despite these criminogenic needs, there are times when people do not qualify for most of them. Yet, they still turn out to be criminals. Take Ted Bundy, for example, the notorious criminal who confessed to killing 30 women in 7 states between 1973 to 1978. He was an exemplary law student who built a relationship with Carole Ann Boone, his wife. People did not see him abuse drugs or alcohol. He was even-tempered with his wife, and he didn't even display antisocial behavior. This is why people never knew he was the murderer for all those years. He was a college-educated and charismatic man. People even describe him as very likable with a good sense of humor.

The only risk factor people may have noticed in his adulthood is his dysfunctional family. His grandmother suffered from depression and agoraphobia, while his grandfather had a raging temper. Archives report that Bundy may have experienced physical or psychological abuse from his grandfather, despite insisting that the two had a good relationship. Because of this, genetics could have played a role in Ted Bundy's behaviors.

After further studies, many of his relatives started to speak about Ted as a kid. Possibly because of trauma and abuse, he started acting strangely around his family. His aunt said that on one occasion, he found Ted placing knives near her as she sleeps. Also, when his mother remarried Johnnie in 1951, Ted was jealous of his mom's new relationship, so he started acting out. As he grew older, he learned to hide these predispositions well to cover his need to kill innocent women.

All of us want criminals to change and adopt a more productive life. Unfortunately, because of their experiences, they may not even have control of their actions. Believe it or not, many people want to change for the better, but they don't know where to start. For us civilians, the best way to deal with these people is to avoid them. But for the system, it's best to innovate more and more ways to identify risk factors of criminal behaviors as early as possible to prevent them before they happen.

Before a Pickpocket Gets to You

You can predict some criminals before they act on their impulses. This gives you a chance to fight or flight. But what about criminals you cannot predict, such as pickpockets? These people swoop in, penetrating your belongings and taking what's yours. Often it will take time before you figure out you're missing something. By that time, the criminal would have already gone. In this segment, let's delve into the minds of pickpockets—one of the most common issues faced by society. Knowing how they think and how they move will help you protect yourself from being victimized. So, how do pickpockets move, and how do you protect yourself from them?

Pickpocketing is one of the most widespread crimes in the world. It is one of the most common because there is a lower risk of getting caught than armed robbers and murderers. Skilled pickpockets can vanish into thin air. You never know where they are or if they're already behind you. They're as slick as foxes, and they make no commotion when they're in action. Believe it or not, a pickpocket down the street can make as much money as those who attempt bank robbery even without putting in much effort. This is why criminals find this an effective and easy way to get money. These people can take your money, gadgets, credit cards, and identification cards in one swoop.

And there's little hope of getting them back. This is bad news for the rest of us. That's why we need to understand more about them to know how to stop them.

According to researchers, there are different levels of pickpocketing in the world. The lowest level consists of simple opportunists. They don't have specific or special techniques in the field, leaving them at risk of getting caught. They target easy people such as those with open bags and those sleeping on benches. The pickpocket simply positions themselves nearby and slowly reaches into the victim's bag. This can only be effective when there's no one else in the scene. But in a crowd, it could be difficult to perform.

A higher level of pickpocketing is targeting wallets. Most people keep their wallets in their side or back pockets. These are more difficult to grab because the person could feel the act. One technique that pickpockets use to grab someone's wallet is to make benign contact. They pretend to bump into you accidentally, so you're focused on the upper side of your body. You neglect to see their hands sliding into your pocket to swipe your wallet. They can cover their hands with their bag or a newspaper to avoid getting caught.

The same method applies in less crowded areas where pickpockets intentionally sandwich you between them. The stalling partner suddenly stops in front of the victim while the "pick" pretends to accidentally bump behind the victim. The stall will apologize to divert the focus of the victim as the "pick" swipes the wallet out.

How does this work?

In the movie "Now You See Me," they reiterated, "The closer you get, the less you see." This means that "magic" happens when people are distracted by something else.

As humans, we tend to focus on one thing and disregard other stimuli in the environment. Little do we know that the real commotion is displayed outside the distracting stimulus. This is how pickpockets take our valuables. And voila! Your belongings are gone without you knowing it.

In the pickpocketing world, all of them are actors. Some pretend to fight in the middle of the crowd while the other "picks" take advantage of the inattentive people. Pickpockets also use children's charm. They instruct kids to show you their toys while they sneak up from behind. Another common trick is intentionally spilling water on the victim's shirt and offering to wipe it off to establish contact and distraction.

The next trick in the book is using sexually appealing people; usually, a woman, to attract others. She will pretend to be drunk and will show affection to other people. Distracted by her sex appeal, the victim is unknowing that the woman is already lifting his wallet or watch. Another trick is "accidentally" dropping coins or papers to get people to help them. While the victim kneels, other members will attempt to steal their wallet.

The last but not the least scheme that pickpockets use is playing the victim. In a crowd, someone might say, "Somebody stole my wallet!" This makes people check if they still have their belongings with them. When they check their bags and pat their pockets, people just showed where their expensive items are, which makes the job of the pickpockets easier.

Seeing how cunning these people are, you need to protect yourself from "picks." One way is to make your valuables difficult to reach. If you are often in a crowded place, wear pants with zippered pockets. When you have a purse or backpack, always secure your belongings in the deepest and most hidden compartment. Better yet, get a money belt so it's difficult for people to take your money.

Another technique you can use is to have a dummy wallet and show it. This way, pickpockets will focus on getting the dummy wallet rather than your actual wallet. It's also important to look confident and secure. Pickpockets can sense confusion and distraction. When they see that you're a tourist, they will most likely target you. So, even when you're new to a place, act as if you belong, like you know where you are going. When you suspect people following you, get inside a secure establishment like a restaurant or a bank, even a police station and wait for them to disappear. You can even report it to the authorities for better protection.

No matter how prepared you are against pickpockets, you still need to be careful. You never know how cunning they can be. So, you always need to be vigilant anywhere you go.

Spotting a Person with Condescending Attitude

Apart from manipulators and criminals, you might also want to avoid people with condescending attitudes. These people need to feel superior among others. Hence, they display arrogance, pride, and hatefulness to other people. Believe it or not, interacting with these people can affect your well-being. Because they tend to degrade people around them, you may start to question yourself, your decisions, and you may experience low self-esteem. In the long run, it could lead to psychological disorders. This is why you need to identify condescending people and protect yourself from them.

Here are signs that people are condescending:

1. Being constantly late
    Everyone values their time, especially busy bees who want to stay productive throughout the day. One of the most common pet peeves of professionals is constantly waiting for people. To them, this means that the person does not respect their time. They could have been more productive. Instead, they end up waiting for other people.

    This is why being constantly late is a sign of having a condescending attitude. These people like to enter the room dramatically to catch attention. In return, they end up wasting people's time.

2. Interrupting others a lot
    This is another manifestation of a condescending attitude. They like interrupting others either to correct their grammar or their pronunciation. Other times, they butt in just to give their opinions, even if others have already stated it.

3. Believing they are better than others
   A classic form of condescending behavior is believing they are better than others. This makes them question others' abilities to accomplish tasks. It makes them take on responsibilities because they believe that if they don't do it, it's not going to be perfect.

4. They cannot accept their mistakes
   Condescending people do not like being corrected. Even when they know they are at fault, they don't want anyone telling them what to do or what to change. To them, giving criticisms and negative feedback about their behavior means stepping on their toes.

5. Believing their status is more important
   These people believe that their life has greater importance. They usually exaggerate their contributions to society so people will think highly of them. And when people share their experiences and achievements, condescending people make it a habit to degrade others' stories to keep their place at the top.

6. They always believe they can
   You can observe condescending people at work when they always say they "can" do it, even if they can't. This results in

unproductivity and work errors that can cause losses and back lags.

7. Despising weak people
When people admit their inability to accomplish some tasks, condescending people show disgust towards these people. Instead of showing empathy and helping others in need, they will give remarks about how that person should have learned more or trained better.

8. Inability to reflect
These people find it difficult to look in the mirror and see themselves for who they really are. They cloud their perceptions towards themselves and fail to recognize their failures and weaknesses.

9. Loves being the center of attention
These people also love being the center of attention. They never fail to turn others' heads even if it means irritating others. Condescending people like to interrupt conversations even if they are not a part of it. They are always late and when they enter the room, they make a scene. And when people are not paying attention to them, they get dramatic to capture people's eyes.

10. Considering everyone as threats or enemies

    Condescending people see everything as a competition. So, even when you're just trying to do your job, these people will see you as a threat. Sometimes, these people even believe that everyone is against them. This is why they seek assurance from others, and they destroy others before it happens to them.

Seeing how draining it is to be with a condescending person, here are strategies you can use to protect yourself from their selfish and egotistical ways.

Don't take it personally. The best way to deal with condescending people is to ignore them and not to take their words personally. This will give you more security, plus they are likely to leave you alone because you are not giving them the position or attention they want.

Call them out. When you're offended by an arrogant person, try calling them out professionally, like "That comment sounds offensive. Do you mind dropping the attitude?" Sometimes, when condescending people get called out, they get surprised that people can stand up to them. And when you can, they may no longer repeat the same mistake.

Neutralize your body language. No matter how irritating they can get, always maintain a neutral body language. This means avoid showing hostility through your facial expressions or behavior. If you do, this will show that arrogant person that they're succeeding. Instead, stand straight and take up your space. And as much as possible, hold your ground and do not shrink back in offense.

Be tactful. When a condescending person starts to attack you for giving criticism or feedback, try clarifying both your goals. You can address the issue by saying, "I want to make sure we're on the same page in improving our efforts to achieve goals. Because how you are acting right now is uncalled for." You can also assure them that you understand how it feels to hear a bad comment. You can say, "I understand how awful it might feel to get a bad review. But that's how we learn." When you put things in a professional tone, that person is more likely to respect you.

Change the subject. As discussed, these people like to be the center of attention. They like to interrupt people while talking, even if the conversation does not involve them. If this happens and they ramble about 'me, me, me,' feel free to change the subject. Direct the spotlight to someone else. Ask them about their achievements or their activities. This will throw the condescending person off and will likely leave you alone.

Keep distance. Perhaps the best way to deal with a condescending person is to avoid them. If they're already in the same room or conversation as you, minimize interacting with them. When they talk to you, just nod and smile. And if it fails, politely excuse yourself from the situation.

Recognize the Body Language of Aggressive Behavior

Despite avoiding these people and changing the subject, some of them can display aggression, which could lead to fights and injuries. This is why it is important to recognize the body language and other nonverbal cues of aggressive behavior so you can predict danger before it happens. Here are some of the most common cues that indicate aggression:

1. Chin up forehead back. You can observe condescending people put their chin high and look down their nose to feel superior. Sometimes, this could be a red flag that someone is willing to resort to aggression.
2. Four degrees. Another red flag is when a person starts to raise their voice. It could mean that they're starting to lose their temper and are starting to get impulsive.

If people keep on provoking, this could lead to a physical fight.

3. Chin thrust. Also known as the jaw clench, this is the act of gritting your teeth and shoving the jaw towards people. When someone does this to you, they are threatening you. It is a nonverbal way of saying back away or else I'll hurt you.

4. Flaring nostrils. This happens when people fan the outer lobes of their noses, so they are as wide as possible. Biologically, when people dilate their noses, it allows more oxygen to enter the lungs. If a person is agitated, they must be filling their lungs to have enough energy to fight.

5. Pursed lips. When people are in tension, you can observe them pursing their lips. But when they are agitated, and they purse their lips, it's a way of saying, "That's the last straw!"

6. Chest puff. When a person is angry, the body gets as wide as possible to assert dominance and strength. It is a way of scaring their opponent to back off before something bad happens.

7. Pupil dilation. Although this is a difficult body language to catch, you still need to

know this when you need it. According to experts, the eyes dilate to capture as many details from the environment as possible. This happens when a person is preparing for a fight. Their eyes dilate to see every weapon, every form of attack, and possible defense strategies.

8. Lowered eyebrows. This is the most common body language that shows aggression. Often, you can even see heads tilted downward. When it's matched with a long, hard stare, it could mean that a person can't wait to lay their hands on you.

9. Teeth-licking. According to experts, human teeth are a primitive weapon we use when we feel threatened. This is why you can observe teeth licking from people who are about to fight. Sometimes, people lick their teeth when their mouth is closed. So, you might see movement on the jaw area or the side of the face that pushes the cheeks and widen it.

10. Blading. Observe boxers in the ring. They use a blading stance in which their bodies turn away to cover their most vulnerable areas. They pull their leg and shoulder back so their attacker can only access the side of the body. Blading

does not only happen in a boxing arena. You can also observe it in real life when people are so agitated, they want to fight.

11. Another common sign of aggression is clenched fists. This indicates anger or dismissal. If you see people clenching their fists, observe how hard they do it because it indicates the severity of their anger.

12. Ocular Orbital tension. When people are doubtful, suspicious, curious, or angry, they narrow their eyes. It could mean that the person heard something offensive, so they tighten their eye muscles as a way of saying, "You did not just say that" or "Watch what you're saying." If the person continues to provoke, it could lead to a fight.

If you observe any of this body language, de-escalate the situation. As much as possible, do not mirror the aggressive body language. Keep your body relaxed and take a step back to give them the emotional space they need. It also helps to show your hands to say to them that you mean no harm non-verbally.

So, you see, manipulators are not the only people you should be worried about. Criminals and condescending people can affect your physical and emotional wellbeing. Remember to review these concepts from time to time as a reminder to protect yourself at all times. If you need any help managing these people, don't hesitate to seek professional guidance. These people can help you decide what to do when people start to affect your life.

Chapter 11 – How the World Sees You

Do You Really See Yourself When You Look in the Mirror?

As we discussed in the previous chapters, body language plays an important role in reading people, understanding what drives them, and predicting their actions. Now that you have learned how to interpret others' non-verbal cues, it's time to focus on your own.

Reading the past chapters, you may have wondered what body language and facial expressions you evoke to the world. You may also ask what posture you do in front of an audience.

Before you learn how to develop your body language, record yourself speaking using your phone or your camera. You can choose a speech on the web which is about three to five minutes long. For this exercise, you don't need to rehearse because it defeats the purpose of seeing the actual body language you evoke in a normal conversation or in public speaking. It would also be best not to use mirrors or phone screens. You should not see yourself while speaking to the camera. This way, you will not control how you act. When positioning the camera, make sure you can see your whole body. Position it front and center to get the best view of yourself while speaking.

After the activity, watch the video once or twice and check the following body languages that apply to you:

- I have a fairly serious expression.
- My body looks pretty still and tense.
- I lean back sometimes.
- I have a reserved posture.
- I seldom smile.
- I smile too much.
- I turn my head away sometimes.
- I often look down.
- I don't spread my eye contact to the audience.
- My hands have minimal movements.
- My hands fidget when I'm nervous
- My hands are clenched.
- My hands are folded
- My hands are in my pocket.
- My hands are rested behind me.
- I keep touching my face.
- My legs are crossed sometimes.
- My legs fidget when I'm nervous.
- I use "uh," "uhm," often.
- My voice is too soft.
- I talk too fast or slow.

- I can't understand some words I'm saying.
- There is no variation in my tone.

If you use any of this body language, don't worry! You're not alone. I, too, didn't know that there was a proper way to interact with people using body language. But with experience and practice, you can improve your public speaking ability and become an effective conduit of motivation and information.

Develop Your Body Language

There is no specific advice on how you can improve your body language due to individual differences. Our minds and bodies are hardwired differently, which is why there is no particular solution for each of us. You already know effective body language. What I can offer you now is tips on how you can tailor-fit the solution to prevent negative body language.

As discussed in the previous chapters, the body and mind are a system. What you feel inside will show on the outside, and it reflects on your body language. When your mind emancipates fear, anxiety, and tension, you will show negative body language. But if your mind is happy, excited, and confident, you will show positive body language. In my years of experience, how you engage with other people depends on your mindset. So, in this chapter, I will be giving you strategies for battling the negativities in your mind and exuding confidence in various situations.

Here are some techniques you can employ:

1. Know your topic.

It is a fact that when you know your topic well, you can increase your chances of delivering your message effectively. With research, you feel more knowledgeable. And if you are knowledgeable, you feel more powerful.

2. Know your audience.

Another important way to feel confident when engaging with people is to know your audience. Professional public speakers always ask the culture and age bracket of their audience all the time. This way, they can tailor their speech to match the interest of their listeners. You can also prevent dead air which could be one of the causes of anxiety. When you know your audience, you can make them relate to your illustrations. Even if there's silence, you can start a topic that they can relate to gather attention. You can use trending apps, movies, and songs. With these, you will observe how they are willing to learn more which gives you success in delivering your message

3. Getting organized.
The next technique to manage your anxiety is to get organized. Carefully plan what you need to say and the sequence of your thoughts. Also, don't forget to prepare the props you need for the presentation. This may include pens and paper, a laptop and projector, and a mic.

To keep yourself on track, use digital tools to engage your audience, such as PowerPoint presentations. Design them strategically to keep it informative and entertaining. It could help if you add movies or clips that can help you get your point across.

4. Practice.
Remember the negative body language you embody. With practice, you can be aware of these non-verbal cues to catch yourself before you show them.

5. Challenge your worries.
When people engage an audience, they might feel that they're not good enough, that people might ridicule them after the speech. These are yet again brought by anxiety, and it will show in your speech. This is why you need to challenge your thoughts as they come. In your thinking

about not being good enough, ask yourself, "What makes you say that? You practiced for how many nights for this event. You can do it."

If you fear that you may be ridiculed after your speech, think that these words are like water off a duck's back. It means that any remark from these people will not affect you unless they are communicated as constructive feedback. In that case, take it positively and act on it for your improvement.

6. Allow yourself to make mistakes.
When you engage an audience, don't be afraid to commit mistakes. Even professional speakers commit mistakes all the time. Sometimes, they never know that they're doing something wrong until after the speech. Because of this, they may receive negative feedback. It could be frustrating at first. But if you look at it proactively, these comments are important to improve your public speaking abilities.

If you catch yourself making a mistake in front of an audience, approach it with humor. You'll be surprised how forgiving and understanding your audience can be. Your audience knows that you're human and that nobody's perfect. So, even if you commit mistakes, it's usually not a big deal to your audience. So, just play with it. Ease your mind. And focus on what is important—that is, getting your message across.

7. Visualize success.
In public speaking, the law of attraction works wonders in the success of an event. If you visualize success, chances are, you will have a more fulfilling result. It makes you trust the process and feel more confident. And even when you feel nervous or terrified on stage, visualizing success will help you push through these barriers. As a result, you can deliver an inspiring and motivating speech.

8. Reward yourself for your successes
When you accomplish a goal, big or small, it is important to reward yourself. This motivates the brain to keep pushing forward despite the challenges. For example, after you completed the activity to identify your body language, reward yourself with rest or food. This will train the brain that there is a prize for every achievement. Instead of feeling demotivated or embarrassed, rewarding

trains your brain to move forward and move to the next task to receive another prize.

It does not matter if your goal is to practice, write your speech, or deliver your speech. It would help if you rewarded your brain to fuel that drive towards success.

9. Deep breathing.
When you feel anxious or terrified, deep breathing is one of the best ways to lower stress in the body. When you inhale deeply, it sends a message to your brain, commanding it to calm down and relax. With practice, you can control your reactions to specific situations and exude confidence to mask the tension you're feeling.

10. Get support.
If you continue to doubt your skills in public speaking, one way to get better is by joining support groups. Some organizations offer public speaking classes and workshops that can help you improve verbal and non-verbal communication.

In these groups, you can see that you're not alone. You can share your fears and weaknesses to get assurance from people. You can learn better approaches to save yourself from blacking out when you make a mistake. Besides that, you will also learn how to deal with hecklers and establish rapport with your audience.

11. Get enough rest.
The last but not the least strategy to improve your confidence while engaging with people is to get enough rest. This is a proven and tested method to relax and energize the brain to prepare it for the event. If a person is well-rested, you can observe more confidence. You can feel them exude a lively and positive vibe. This is because sleeping normalizes the hormones in your body that affect how you act and react. These include the following:

Endorphins. These are hormones released by your glands that help relieve stress and pain.
Serotonin. Also known as the happy hormone, serotonin is the key to organize your mood and promote feelings of happiness It also enables

brain cells and other nervous system cells to communicate with each other efficiently.

Cortisol. Sleep also normalizes cortisol in the body, also known as the stress hormone. With balance, you can reduce feelings of anxiety and apprehension which can help you achieve success when dealing with a crowd.

What if You Have an RBF?

I know what you might be thinking right now. What if I have a resting bitch face? Don't worry! I have some tricks to improve it. But first, let's discuss the psychology of RBF or resting Bitch face.

RBF is a cultural advent that describes a facial expression conveying a particular mix of judgment, boredom, and irritation. The worst part is people have no idea that they have the face. They don't even know that they are warding people off because of the ingrained expression on their faces. Because of this, others think they are unapproachable and mean. This can affect how one builds relationships and rapport with people.

Unfortunately, researchers still have no idea about the cause of RBF. Some say that it is just how their face is formed. Others, however, claim that it is a learned trait to ward off unwanted people. But because they do it often, they embodied the face and made it a habit. Whatever the case is, you need to learn how to manage your resting bitch face to look more approachable, especially when dealing with clients, customers, and listeners. Here are some techniques:

1. When looking at someone, look up at them. Raise your head, so your eyes look more open and less intimidating.

2. You can also use makeup to reshape downcast eyes. You can use eyeliner and eye shadow to draw more attention to your upper eyes and make them look welcoming.

3. Another technique is replacing that frown with a small smile. It would help if you exercise the muscles around your mouth. Smile in front of the mirror for 20 seconds when you wake in the morning and before you sleep at night. This accustoms your muscles to this behavior, so you can display it in public like it's your nature.

4. Use the eyebrow flash. When you arch your brows upward, it is a non-verbal way of saying, "Hi! I recognize you, and I'm friendly." This makes you exude a warmer and more welcoming vibe.

5. You can also try accessorizing and wearing brighter clothing. This can help counteract your unapproachable face and allows your body to exude liveliness

Once you apply the strategies, try re-recording yourself with the same speech. You should observe a major difference in how you hold yourself in front of the camera. Remember practice, practice, practice. Even when it feels difficult and challenging, break free from your limits and keep moving forward.

Don't Let Anything Give You Away

Aside from delivering speeches, you can also use the techniques above when interacting in other situations like debates, arguments, or meetings, professional or casual ones. During these times, you cannot avoid dealing with condescending people. Knowing how they act, expect to be ridiculed, provoked, agitated, and insulted. Despite this, you need to keep your composure and focus on what matters. Because if you let them get under your skin, they could turn the situation around and make you seem like the unprofessional one.

So how do you deal with condescending people in social interactions without losing your calm composure?

One technique you can use is putting up a poker face. This is an effective way to maintain an emotionless, apathetic demeanor, especially when dealing with arrogant and narcissistic people. Once you master the poker face, people cannot affect how you respond to the whole situation. You control what you say and what you do despite the agitation that people cause. This is important to maintain a neutral demeanor that shows people that you can be professional despite the challenges presented to you. This will also shed light on the real instigator so the head of the meeting can call them out.

So, how do you present a poker face? Here are some techniques.

1. Maintain neutral body language.
    This means avoiding any negative cues that may give you away. No matter how much you want to roll your eyes, don't do it. The instigator will notice it and add more flair to the situation. When you're being agitated in a meeting, relax your face. Don't give a snark, a smile, or a frown.

    You also need to watch your hands and legs. As usual, do not cross them and do not clench your fists. If there's a table, it's important to show your hands to make

260

people feel that you can still trust them. If you have a pen, hold onto it. It could help control any hand twitches that could give you away.

2. Keep blinking.
   Often, when people hear surprising news, they neglect to blink. Don't make the same mistake. Catch yourself when you're not blinking and blink normally as if you heard nothing.

3. Look away.
   When difficult people face you, direct your eyes to another subject to allow your brain to process the situation and gather your composure. If the instigator requires to be looked eye to eye, focus your sight on their forehead. This way, you can hide any sudden movement of the eyes that can give you away.

4. Bite your tongue. Even if you feel like speaking up when it's not your turn, don't do it. If you have pent-up feelings or thoughts, there is a great tendency that you'll spill them like tea. There can be incoherence, and you may not deliver your message effectively, which can only confuse your audience. Instead, bite your tongue. It shouldn't be too hard, so

it bleeds. But bite it strong enough to remind yourself to keep your cool.

5. Always stay the positive route.
   When everything gets too overwhelming or if you need to respond, always take the positive route. Even when you feel like you've been beaten down or when you feel agitated, always exude a level of positivity. Don't forget to smile, acknowledge others' opinions, and say 'thank you.'

   In the eyes of your bosses and other experts, this is a form of professionalism. It gives them the impression that you take criticism and feedback constructively. It also says a lot of things about your personality. Other people can infer that you have a high tolerance for condescending people, and you like taking the high road rather than stooping to their level. So, even if you feel hurt or degraded, you still win the battle because now, your boss trusts you and is confident about you. This means the plan of the instigator did not work.

There you have it! These are some of the most common techniques to alleviate anxiety and promote positive body language. With practice, you can exude positivity and confidence that can help you succeed in your presentations, meetings, promotions, debates, and many more. With these strategies, you can ignore hecklers and maintain a professional composure no matter how challenging the situation is. In time, you will observe that learning to control your body language works wonders. It can help you succeed in all the facets of your life.

Chapter 12 – Using Body Language to Become the Person You Want to Be

Body language is critical in communication. The right gestures and behavior during a conversation will help you get your message across more efficiently than words. Studies show that 60-90% of all communication is non-verbal.

The way you present yourself for the first few minutes is critical in making a lasting impression. Here are some techniques in mastering the art of body language to help you become the person you want to be.

The Best Kind of Handshake

Different countries have varying greeting customs. But a handshake is internationally recognized as the standard formal greeting gesture. Unbeknownst to some people, this practice has been around since the 5th Century BC in Greece. It was a gesture indicating peaceful intentions as it shows that both people do not carry weapons in their hands.

Much has changed over the years, but the handshake was passed down to this modern era. Today, most job interviews and business meetings start with a handshake. It has even become a gauge for initially assessing a person's character and personality. As well as a symbolic seal of a deal, promise, or commitment. Hence, the importance of having a good handshake.

These are the best handshakes that convey a positive personality:

Equality Handshake

Though some people mistakenly believe that a strong handshake conveys a strong personality, it does not. It only presents you as dominant and authoritative. Another form of the dominant handshake is a palm-down thrust with the other person's palm facing up. During job interviews and business negotiations, this is certainly not what you would want to project.

When shaking a person's hand, it's always good to express equality as it shows respect and encourages trust. In a proper handshake, both person's hands should be vertical. Modulate the pressure of your grip to match the other person's grip.

Double Handler Handshake

The double handler handshake is also known as the politician's handshake. It is a powerful handshake that conveys sincerity and a strong bond. This involves placing the left hand over the right and cupping the clasped hands.

This handshake can be used when you find yourself on the other end of a dominant handshake. When a person offers you a palm-down thrust, respond with a palm-up handshake. Then, use your other hand to clasp and straighten your palms vertically.

This also works for a bone breaker and lingering handshakes. By clasping your other hand over the handshake, you are signaling the other person to let go of your hand.

It is important to know that handshaking is more than just handshaking. The perfect handshake must be accompanied by these elements:

Eye Contact

Handshake extends to the eyes. Looking at the person in the eyes conveys passion, respect, and sincerity. Eye contact is said to activate the secretion of oxytocin or what is otherwise known as the love hormone. This hormone gives people the feeling of well-being and connection. Making eye contact during a handshake, lays out the foundation of rapport between two people.

Firm Grip

A firm grip shows confidence and strength. A firm grip involves moderate pressure and an unrushed clasp. A hasty handshake can appear disrespectful. Clasp the other person's hand with your fingers and lock your thumbs with theirs.

Moderate Shake

A good handshake can go up to three small pumps. Beyond that will make you look overly excited. Release the person's hand after the shake. A lingering handshake can be very awkward especially if it's with a person you are not close with. You also have to remember that shaking doesn't mean yanking. Do not pull or yank the person's hand. Shake it up and down by lifting your hands by the elbows.

Verbal Introduction

Use words in conjunction with the handshake. Introduce yourself and offer a greeting. This will further give the impression of confidence. You can say a few compliments but do not gush over the person so as not to make them uncomfortable. Remember the person's name and use it when addressing them. This shows that you care and projects a positive impression.

A good confident handshake can be achieved with constant practice. You can rehearse shaking hands with some friends and family and asking them what their impressions are based on the handshake.

Does Mirroring Work?

The human brain is hardwired to mirror the behavior of people we like in what is called limbic synchrony. As early as infancy, babies' heartbeats tend to synchronize with the person they are closest to—their mothers. This is why children often mimic the behavior of people around them and establish connections with body movements.

Mirroring was first discovered in the early 90s by a group of researchers in Italy. Oddly enough, they were studying macaque monkeys. According to accounts, one researcher was reaching for his food when he noticed that some neurons of the monkey fired up. The monkey's brain is unable to differentiate between doing it and seeing it be done. This is when they accidentally stumbled on what was later called the mirror neurons.

Most of the time we are unaware that we are mirroring people we like or are attracted to. And in the same way, we unconsciously gravitate towards someone that mirrors our behavior. Mirroring has proven to be a very effective tool when you want to influence someone. For the past decades, politicians and businessmen have recognized the value of mirroring behavior. This is also true in dating, men and women are likely to mirror the actions of a person they are interested in.

If done correctly, mirroring can be a powerful persuasive technique. Let's take a look at some tips to help you use the mirroring technique to your advantage.

Nonverbal Mirroring

The first thing to do is to establish a foundation for rapport by starting with what is called fronting. Face the other person squarely whether you are standing or sitting. Positioning your body towards them shows that you are giving them your full attention.

Next is eye contact. It's an effective technique in establishing a connection. This is backed up by science. According to one study, making eye contact releases oxytocin which is necessary for forming social bonds. But it can be very tricky; too much eye contact can make the other person feel awkward.

Another essential nonverbal element that is useful in the mirroring technique is the triple nod. Try slowly nodding three times and tilting your head when a person is speaking. People like to be listened to. This does not only show that you are agreeing with what they are saying but you are also conveying empathy towards their feelings. This makes them feel understood on a deeper level and more likely to feel warm towards you.

After establishing a connection, mirror their body language, gesture, and even facial expression. Cross your legs when the other person crosses their legs. Some people constantly raise their eyebrows or gesture with their hands when making a point. Copy their gestures but do not be too obvious otherwise it will backfire on you. You must also remember to steer away from mirroring negative body language like folding the arms and looking away. Reflect only actions that convey interest and positive energy toward the person you are talking to.

Vocal Mirroring

Mirroring is much more than just copying physical actions. It extends to mimicking all nonverbal aspects. Have you ever noticed two close friends who are talking to each other? The tone, pitch, speed, and volume of their voices gradually mimic each other. This phenomenon is called phonetic convergence.

Match the cadence of the person's speech. Vocal cadence is the rhythm or flow of a person's speech. A person's cadence is unique and can be affected by what they are feeling at that moment. They can speak slowly, monotonously, soothingly, excitedly, or animatedly. By mimicking a person's vocal pace and volume, you also mirror their emotions which makes you more likable.

Again, the mimicry should be subtle. Do not ever try to copy the person's accent. This can be very disastrous and appear insulting when done incorrectly.

Verbal Mirroring

Research shows that waitresses and salespeople who repeat the customer's words get a higher tip and close more deals. People have certain words and phrases that they use too often. When talking to a person try listening to slang and quotes that they like to repeat and integrate these into your speech. To avoid being obvious, you can rephrase.

You can test if a person has warmed up to your mirroring technique by checking if they mirror you back. Make an overt action that is unrelated to your conversation like scratching your nose and seeing if they copy you.

Mirroring is a function of the brain and has been proven to be an effective technique countless times. We are attracted to people who look and act like us. In the late '80s, one researcher suggested that couples who have been together for a long time tend to look alike over time. But an opposing theory has recently surfaced claiming that couple's faces do not gradually become similar. Instead, they have always been similar. The Similar/Attraction Theory posits a person will more likely be attracted to another person who has similar qualities than a person who does not.

7 Effective Ways to Show Your Confidence

Confidence is knowing and believing in yourself and your abilities. Confidence does not mean that you feel superior to other people. Instead, it's a feeling of security of knowing that you are capable of overcoming things and succeeding. It makes you feel ready for what life throws at you.

In work settings and relationship settings, confidence plays an important role. Confident people will stand out during job interviews and are more likely to land promotions. Confidence gives you more influence among your peers.

Some people grow up to be naturally timid and reserved, but it doesn't mean that they cannot learn to look and appear confident. Confidence is not a born trait. It is a skill that is learned over time through practice. Here are some ways to project confidence.

1. Assume a Confident Posture

Posture says a lot about a person. When a person sits slumped and hunched, it gives the perception of weakness, fear, and shame. But when a person stands tall and sits upright, they communicate a strong confident personality.

To assume a confident stance, align your legs with your shoulders. With both arms hanging loose on your sides or your hips. Relax your shoulders, lean back a little, and open up your chest. Slightly raise your chin. When sitting down, you can cross your legs and lean back on the backrest. Use the armrest if there are any or place both hands on your lap.

You should stand tall but not uncomfortably upright. Your posture should feel and look natural otherwise you will appear uptight and tense.

Face the person squarely and point your feet towards them. Doing this expresses interest which will make you feel rewarding to talk to. Refrain from actions that make other people think you have to go somewhere or wish that you are somewhere else.

2. Work on your Eye Contact

Eye contact goes a long way to show confidence and respect to the people you are interacting with. Avoiding eye contact can convey anxiety, shame, and doubt. For some people, making eye contact can be uncomfortable. To manage this, you can use the time-tested solution of focusing on the space between the person's eyebrows. Avoid focusing your gaze on a person's mouth, nose, or peculiar marks on their faces as this can be perceived as offensive.

3. Use Mirroring Technique

Mirroring can be key to connecting with people. Behaving and looking like them will increase the chances of acceptance and understanding between you. When the person is excited about something, it's good to match their energy and enthusiasm in the same subject. Copy their tone of voice and use similar words to what they use. Mirroring is an art that is accompanied by subtlety and if applied properly can greatly increase your influence over others.

4. Be conscious of Your Hands

The way you hold your hands can show the level of confidence you have. Wringing your hands makes you look nervous and anxious. Sticking them in your pockets shows you're reserved and doubtful. Crossing them over your chest or holding them over your belly projects defensiveness and discomfort.

To avoid negative perceptions, just let your arms hang naturally by your sides. If you are holding a phone or a bag, hold them at waist level. You can stick your thumbs in your pockets and let your other finger point downwards.

Hand gestures are also a critical part of body language. One of the most positively recognized hand gestures is the steeple hand gesture. Place your fingertips together to form a point. Spread your fingers and arch them to form the shape of a church steeple. It's a powerful gesture that shows commitment and sincerity to what you are saying.

Another hand gesture is the palms up or rogatory hand position. Here the person offers up their open palms as they speak. It gives people the impression of openness, compliance, humility, and cooperation. It is often used by politicians as a subtle way of saying, "My hands are clean" or "I am at your service".

When presenting, avoid pointing your index fingers. While this may show passion, it can often be offensive. Gesture and point with your palms instead. This way you appear more composed and poised.

5. Avoid Fidgeting

We all have that thing that we do when we're nervous. It can be tapping our fingers or feet, jingling coins in our pockets, or shifting our weight when seated and uncrossing and crossing our legs. These show a lack of confidence and can be very distracting to the person you are talking to.

For some people fidgeting has become a habit. To counter this, you must recognize your triggers and try to avoid them. Focus your mind on the conversation and task at hand.

6. Pay attention to your voice and facial expression

Study your facial expressions in the mirror. Look at what your normal face looks like and what it conveys. Some people have very stern faces that make them appear angry even if they aren't. Others have unsmiling faces that make them unapproachable. These make it hard for you to communicate your emotions effectively. Smiling and putting on a pleasant face will naturally make you sound pleasant, inviting, and confident.

The way you speak is as important as what you say. Avoid stammering and using fillers like "um" and "uh". Never use the question inflection. It makes you sound unsure. Speak with conviction and confidence. Let the words flow smoothly and look the person in the eyes while speaking.

7. Use Power poses

A decade ago, Amy Cuddy fueled the power pose craze. She claimed that assuming a superman or wonder woman pose for a few minutes increases your confidence. Her theory was that our body language affects what we think about ourselves and our abilities. Hence, by assuming a powerful stance we also feel more powerful.

Taking Full Control of Your Life

Life is so uncertain. No matter how much planning we do, it just doesn't go as planned. No matter how much work you put in, you just don't get to where you want to go. No matter how persistent we try to be, the world seems to just fling endless challenges in our direction. Like it doesn't want us to succeed—to be happy. This is when life becomes unfair and confusing. We start to lose a sense of what we are doing and where we are going.

Other times we feel like we make wrong decisions after wrong decisions and we lose confidence in our wisdom. So, we trust other people's opinions more than our own to be the right opinion. We start to believe that they know better than us because they made the right decisions with their lives.

We can see this in family settings where children are told that mothers always know what is best for their children. And while this may be true for some moms and younger kids, it's not always the case for everyone. Some of us grew up in a toxic family environment. We have family members who compete with us and do not want to see us succeed. The same goes for some friends and colleagues.

Accepting advice is a sign of maturity as we give recognition to the fact that we still have a lot to learn about life. But we should never entrust our lives with someone else. Though it might seem to be an easier option when we are faced with a dilemma, it also means relinquishing control of our lives. If we let this happen, our life is not ours but someone else's version of what our life should be. We are sacrificing our authenticity and individuality. We become drifters, alive but not living.

So how can we take back control?

Acceptance

First, you need to deal with the regret for the time that you lost. Come to peace with every wrong decision you made. Accept that not everything in life is predictable. Acceptance does not mean surrender. Resisting things that are out of your control will not change anything and will only hurt you more. Instead of trying to change the scenario, try changing how you deal with it. Change your attitude towards it and think of ways to make the best out of a bad situation.

Set your goals

Shift your focus to your needs by setting new goals. Visualize not just where you want your life to go but how it should be in the present. Prepare for the unexpected but focus on the things within your circle of influence. Your time is your most valuable asset. Use it for things that will benefit you and help you achieve your goals. Outlining your goals will enable you to direct your life where you want it to go, giving you a feeling of control.

Come Up with Alternative Plans

Planning should always include a contingency plan. And when possible, try to prevent situations that you don't want to happen. We have already established that not everything will go smoothly. Think of the worst-case scenario and deliberate all possible alternative actions. When you encounter a small failure, you usually decide and act on impulse and emotion. Having an alternative plan will help you deal with setbacks and help you get back on track.

Recognize your self-worth

We all need validation whether for our abilities or looks. When we fail to receive it from people we love and admire, it weakens our confidence and self-worth. People who truly care and love you will encourage your growth and self-esteem. Selfish and manipulative people will engage in withholding behavior. They will continually refuse to recognize your positive qualities.

To counter this, do not be reliant on others' validation. Recognize your self-worth. Believe in your abilities—in what you can do and what you can become. Encourage yourself. You are your own person. You are perfectly imperfect.

Create Your Moment

A lot of times, we feel trapped or out of control because of other people's actions or inaction. They can disagree with us and fail to see how we think certain things should be done. When you feel stuck in the same position for a long time, it's time to start thinking of ways to change the setting.

Take this work scenario for example. Penny has been working in a company for ten years and has applied for promotion many times, but her boss has appointed someone else every time. Penny begins to doubt her abilities which affects her self-esteem and self-worth.

Instead of being depressed. Penny can seek places where she will feel secure and appreciated. Penny can request a transfer to another department where there is a different boss and more opportunities. She can also start a small side business in which she feels passionate. Then she can quit her job, once the business is doing well.

Sometimes, we are not given the same opportunities as others. This is why we need to create and seize our moments.

Associate Selectively

It's important to remember that the people we associate with have a big influence on what we do and how we feel and act. Your life will become better and healthier if you surround yourself with positive and supportive people. Distance yourself from people who give you a negative feeling or make you act in opposition to your values. Disentangle yourself from toxic, one-sided, and limiting relationships.

Recent studies show that exposure to social media has a great impact on how we behave and view ourselves. People who interact on social media often reportedly feel more insecure, anxious, and jealous. Social media leads some people to feel depressed from comparing their lives with others. It lets people set an unachievable standard for how they should look and behave. Also, social media lets you project the best digital version of yourself. This can be good for expressing oneself, but it can foster negative feelings when a person realizes it's all just an illusion.

The bottom line is you should hang out with the right people and expose yourself to the right environment. This will greatly improve your mood, attitude, and outlook on life making you happier and more productive.

Conclusion

Dealing with narcissists, liars, manipulators, criminals, and condescending people is an inevitable part of life. So, if we cannot avoid them, the best thing to do is to protect ourselves from being victimized by them.

In this book, we discussed the effects of long-term manipulation and exposure to arrogant people. It can lead to self-doubt, anxiety, passivity, unproductivity, depression, shame, and guilt. Seeing how severe the consequences are, there is a need to learn how the body reacts and how it communicates. Understanding this will give you insight into interpreting one's body language. But then again, it is important to create your baseline before you start reading other people's non-verbal cues. This baseline will allow you to interpret body language more accurately. With this guide, you can identify the normal behavior and body language of people and spot sudden changes which could indicate lying or deception.

We also discussed how humans communicate verbally and non-verbally. In the past chapters, we tackled some of the strategies to improve verbal communication and nonverbal communication. Both of which are important to convey a message effectively to your audience. To give you a more detailed guide, we have discussed the types of non-verbal cues such as gestures, posture, proxemics, oculesics, and haptics. Studying these will help you interpret their meanings. Plus, it can help you understand what nonverbal cues are appropriate in specific situations. We also discussed how to avoid miscommunication. A huge factor of it is considering one's culture. Remember that body language which is common in your country may not be appropriate to others. This is why it is crucial to become culturally sensitive. It promotes respect and understanding among people despite their race and beliefs.

We also learned the different body languages and their specific indications. While ascribing meaning to individual body language can give you a hint about one's intentions, it would help if you read body language as a whole. This is why it is important to remember the concepts about posture and its impact. In this book, we also discussed open and closed posture which can tell you a lot about a person's intentions and personality.

Aside from posture, considering proxemics is also necessary to show respect to other people. As discussed, there are four main levels of distance that depend on the relationship of people. The closest distance is intimate distance which is shared by couples and spouses. The second level is personal distance shared by close friends and family. This is about 1.5 feet to 4 feet. The third level is social distance shared by acquaintances. And lastly, public distance is used in public speaking. Always remember to identify the relationship so you can determine the proper distance you need to maintain with the people you're interacting with.

After these topics, we also talked about liars, the types of liars, and their reasons for lying. Seeing how detrimental it is to be victimized by liars, it is important to remember the most common ways to spot a liar. Watch out when a person moves their head quickly and when their breathing starts to change. You can also observe that they blink more often, or they don't blink at all. These are only some of the signs that you may be dealing with a liar. Review these concepts from time to time to protect yourself from deception in your daily interactions.

Another important topic we discussed in this book is liars who hide behind their computer screens. Without knowledge about these people, you may become a victim of a scam, identity theft, and many more. Always remember how you can determine when a person is lying over the web or over the phone.

This will help you ignore or take action against people who attempt to scam you.

The next enticing topic we discussed was speed-reading people. This is the process of gathering as much information about a person's intentions at first glance. Speed-reading is important to remember, especially when people try to take advantage of your feelings and hectic schedules. By learning how to speed-read people, you can already think about your reaction so you can act before you get victimized.

Since part of speed-reading is considering people's emotions, it's also important to become emotionally intelligent. This is one's ability to recognize and manage one's emotions. Many people discount the importance of EQ. Little do they know that this plays a role in the achievement of success. Aside from this, it also helps people achieve peace and true happiness in life. It also grants protection against people who try to instigate or cause any trouble.

We also discussed manipulation, its risk factors, and its determinants. These factors help you identify manipulators and manage them as soon as possible. Unfortunately, these are not the only people you need to deal with in your daily life. Some are criminals who can do far worse than manipulators while others are condescending people who try to demean you to feel more superior. Emotional intelligence, matched with the ability to discern warning signs, can help you avoid the damaging and detrimental actions these people may commit against you.

After you have learned how to read people's actions and predict their behavior before it happens, you also learned how to focus on your own body language and how to improve it. In this book, we discussed positive and negative body language that can affect your presentation and interaction with other people. In the latter part, we tackled how to monitor the body language you evoke to the world and how you improve it to make communication more effective. With practice and determination, you will observe that body language matched with high emotional intelligence can grant success in various aspects of life.

If you've been a victim of manipulation and you feel doubt, shame, and guilt, you now have an opportunity to do something with your life. Don't let yourself succumb to the toxicity of your relationships. Apply what you have learned and slowly break free from the chains that have been holding you back. Use this book as your weapon, as your guide to cutting ties from toxic people in building relationships with healthier ones. Let this be a beacon that gives you direction to the help you need so you can heal and slowly rise from the ashes. In no time, I guarantee you will become a more empowered individual. Now that you know what to do, it's time to make a move.

www.ingramcontent.com/pod-product-compliance
Lightning Source LLC
Chambersburg PA
CBHW022046020426
42335CB00012B/565